West Riding Steam

DEREK HUNTRISS

Never Again Publishing

First Published in 2019 by Never Again Publishing

Copyright © Derek Huntriss

ISBN 978-1-9160733-0-2

Printed in Poland by LF Book Services Ltd (www.lfbookservices.co.uk)

Front Cover: The parting of the L&Y and GN routes out of Bradford Exchange was controlled by St. Dunstan's signal box. Behind the box are the lines to Halifax with Stanier 2-6-4T No.42616 passing the site of St. Dunstan's station on the line to Leeds. It is working the 10.5am Bradford portion of the 'Devonian' on 2nd June 1967. No.42616 had only recently been reallocated from Birkenhead MPD where it had seen use on Birkenhead to Chester services. The station at St. Dunstan's had closed on 15th September 1952. *Peter Fitton*

Title page: Whilst many services over former Great Central lines in the West Riding were in the hands of electric traction following the electrification of the Woodhead route, trains heading east over the former MS&L main line were still in the hands of steam. Here Ex-LNER Class B1 4-6-0 No.61063 stands in Sheffield Victoria station on 20th April 1958. *W.Potter/Kidderminster Railway Museum*

Back Cover: During the summer service of 1967 Jubilee 4-6-0s were booked to work the 6.40am Birmingham to Glasgow which they worked from Leeds City. Here No.45562 *Alberta* crosses the infant river Ribble near Stainforth on 12 August. *Derek Huntriss*

Introduction

Stretching from Ais Gill in the north to Sheffield in the south and from Goole in the east to Saddleworth in the west, the West Riding of Yorkshire could be described as a county of marked contrasts: having some of the most inhospitable landscape that England can offer and possessing two major centres of traditional industry. At the time they were the textile industry around Leeds and Bradford as well as the iron and steel industries centred around Sheffield and Rotherham. From the estuary of the Humber where the docks at Goole were in the county, almost across to the Irish Sea and within its broad acres there was much rich agricultural land. To support this microcosm which it could be said represented the whole of England, it had the additional advantage of being located above one of the richest coalfields in the country.

To support these infant industries were a number of mineral lines which were to play a crucial role in the developing railways of the region. The first of these was the Middleton Colliery Railway in Leeds. The Middleton Colliery Railway made history right from the start. To protect its route, the land-and coal-owner Charles Brandling secured an Act of Parliament: the very first Act titled for, and largely concerned with, the building of a waggonway or railway. From its opening in September 1758, horses pulled thousands of tons of coal a year down the waggonway to Leeds. Cheaper coal prices, based on more efficient transport, gave Leeds a head start in the newly developing large-scale industries. From these beginnings it was a short step towards the construction of lines for both freight and passenger services. Eventually the West Riding sported no less than seven major railway companies, eleven significant joint lines and a small number of minor systems. A number of these lines were built in direct competition and fought long battles, waged major campaigns and incessantly vied with each other for supremacy, only cooperating when no other course of action remained.

The Grouping of 1923 should have put an end to the years of fierce competition but in fact it miserably failed to do so. The Lancashire & Yorkshire and London & North Western together with the Midland became part of the London, Midland and Scottish Railway whilst the Great Northern, Great Central, North Eastern and the Hull & Barnsley were absorbed into the London & North Eastern Railway. Although a number of company's lines met their demise before Nationalisation in 1948, these were relatively few. The onset of BR meant that there were ever declining finances and closures became more common. Having been the battle-ground for a number of the pre-grouping companies the West Riding eventually fell into three BR regions, the London Midland, Eastern and North Eastern Regions and as time moved on the regional boundaries were changed with both lines amd motive power depots passing from one region to another.

For the railway enthusiast this area where steam had reigned, the final rites were not seen until the end of 1967, and into 1968 steam still worked in from other regions. This title first takes the reader over the Settle and Carlisle route from Ais Gill and then on to Skipton with a deviation to the 'Little' North Western to Clapham. The short branch line to Barnoldswick is illustrated before a more in depth look at the Grassington branch and the now preserved line from Keighley to Oxenhope. The Queensbury Triangle is also illustrated before a visit to the Lancashire & Yorkshire Railway's route from Summit tunnel to Normanton also with images depicting the challenging route from Todmorden to Copy Pit summit, the last station being at Portsmouth before the line crossed the county boundary into Lancashire.

Images taken on the former LNWR route over Standedge commence on Saddleworth viaduct and continue through the Colne valley through to Huddersfield with a glimpse of the Meltham branch and the spectacular Longwood viaduct. A visit to the industrial conurbation of Bradford begins at Shipley and examines Manningham depot before arriving at Forster Square station. The steep climb out of Bradford Exchange sees locos working hard up the grade to

St. Dunstans and Laisterdyke. We take a brief look at operations in Halifax before moving over to Leeds where we look at the once complex network of lines that supported the competing business fought over by the pre-Grouping companies.

Covering the lines north and esst of Leeds locations include Harrogate, Pateley Bridge, Wetherby and Tadcaster with visits to Selby, Goole and Church Fenton before arriving at York. Here we see archive images featuring a Class A8 4-6-2 tank and a Class J21 at Layerthorpe before arriving at Donaster in time for the celebrations of Doncaster's centenary in 1953 when a pair of Ivatt Atlantics are seen arriving with a special from King's Cross which had been organised by Alan Pegler. Also a number of locos have been specially prepared for public viewing. After observing operations around Wakefield we journey south through Royston Junction and visits are also made to Hare Park Junction, Mexborough and Barnsley and after a brief look at Silkstone and Dodworth we arrive in Sheffield. Here we are privileged to admire the work of Derek Penney whose efforts to capture moving steam on 8 ASA Kodachrome film have been carefully enhanced with Photoshop. As well as Jubilee-hauled trains on the climb out of Sheffield Midland up to Dore & Totley we visit the former Great Central station at Victoria where Directors, K3s as well as B17s on the Liverpool to Harwich boat trains have been captured.

This compilation is dedicated to the late Gerald Dixon (Gerry to his friends), respected architect and railway photographer. Born in the Falkland islands he moved 'home' (as it was then described) to the UK in 1939 and eventually gained his RIBA qualifications in 1956. In the 1962-64 period he joined the Warwickshire Railway Society on many of their shed visits, as well as commencing his own longer distance trips. Thereafter, he made regular visits to the north of England, the West Riding in particular, where he found the architectural merits of the region amongst the industrialised scenic landscape very appealing. By then he had acquired a 35mm Pentax, plus telephoto lens, and his chance meeting with members of the MNA at Holbeck shed in February 1967 led to both an increase in activities and the opportunity for more car chases. Forty of his mainly unpublished images are seen here for the first time.

As always, deepest thanks are offered to all other photographers whose work recorded the railway scene in the West Riding over 50 years ago. Without their efforts this title could not have been contemplated. The railway tickets seen in this title are from 'The Darwin Collection' and the maps are by Roger Smith.

Derek Huntriss
Coventry
April 2019

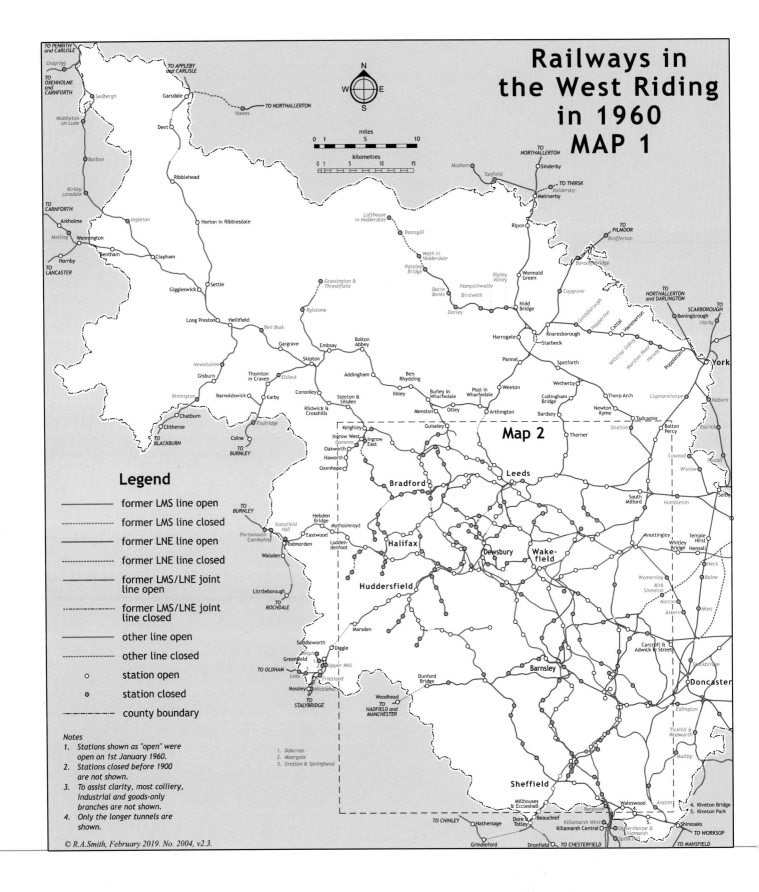

Railways in the West Riding in 1960 MAP 1

TO PENRITH and CARLISLE
Grayrigg
TO OXENHOLME and CARNFORTH
Sedbergh
TO APPLEBY and CARLISLE
Garsdale
Middleton on Lune
TO NORTHALLERTON
Hawes
Dent
Barbon
Ribblehead
Kirkby Lonsdale
TO CARNFORTH
Arkholme
Ingleton
Horton in Ribblesdale
Melling
Wennington
Hornby
Bentham
TO LANCASTER
Clapham
Giggleswick
Settle
Long Preston
Hellifield
Gargrave
Newsholme
Skipton
Gisburn
Thornton in Craven
Elslack
Barnoldswick
Earby
Rimington
Chatburn
Clitheroe
TO BLACKBURN
Colne
TO BURNLEY
Foulridge
Bell Busk

Masham
Tanfield
Sinderby
TO NORTHALLERTON
Baldersby
TO THIRSK
Melmerby
Lofthouse in Nidderdale
Ramsgill
Ripon
TO PILMOOR
Brafferton
Wath in Nidderdale
Pateley Bridge
Dacre Banks
Hampsthwaite
Birstwith
Ripley Valley
Wormald Green
Boroughbridge
TO NORTHALLERTON and DARLINGTON
Copgrove
Darley
Nidd Bridge
Goldsborough
Hopperton
Cattal
Hammerton
TO SCARBOROUGH
Beningbrough
Harby
Harrogate
Knaresborough
Starbeck
Wilstrop Siding
Marston Moor
Hessay
Poppleton
York
Pannal
Spofforth
Weeton
Wetherby
Collingham Bridge
Thorp Arch
Copmanthorpe
Naburn
Menston
Otley
Arthington
Bardsey
Newton Kyme
Tadcaster
Stutton
Bolton Percy
Escrick

Grassington & Threshfield
Rylstone
Embsay
Bolton Abbey
Addingham
Ben Rhydding
Ilkley
Burley in Wharfedale
Pool in Wharfedale
Cononley
Steeton & Silsden
Kildwick & Crosshills
Keighley
Guiseley
Map 2
Thorner
Cawood
Wistow
Recall

Ingrow West
Damems
Ingrow East
Oakworth
Haworth
Oxenhope
Bradford
Leeds
South Milford
Hambleton
Selby

TO BURNLEY
Hebden Bridge
Stansfield Hall
Mytholmroyd
Portsmouth
Cornholme
Eastwood
Todmorden
Luddenfoot
Halifax
Dewsbury
Wakefield
Knottingley
Whitley Bridge
Temple Hirst
Hensall
Heck
Balne
Womersley
Kirk Smeaton
Norton
Moss
Askern

Walsden
Huddersfield
Litrtleborough
TO ROCHDALE
Marsden
Dunford Bridge
Barnsley
Carcroft & Adwick le Street
Stockbridge
Doncaster

Saddleworth
Delph
Diggle
Greenfield
Upper Mill
TO OLDHAM
Lees
Frizland
Mossley
Mickelhurst
TO STALYBRIDGE
Woodhead
TO HADFIELD and MANCHESTER
Edlington
Tickhill & Wadworth
Maltby

Sheffield
Millhouses & Ecclesall
Waleswood
Anston
4. Kiveton Bridge
5. Kiveton Park
TO CHINLEY
Hathersage
Dore & Totley
Beauchief
Beighton
Killamarsh West
Killamarsh Central
Upperthorpe & Killamarsh
Spink Hill
Shireoaks
TO WORKSOP
Grindleford
Dronfield
TO CHESTERFIELD
TO MANSFIELD

1. Dobcross
2. Moorgate
3. Grotton & Springhead

Legend

— former LMS line open
---- former LMS line closed
— former LNE line open
---- former LNE line closed
— former LMS/LNE joint line open
---- former LMS/LNE joint line closed
— other line open
---- other line closed
○ station open
◉ station closed
----- county boundary

Notes

1. Stations shown as "open" were open on 1st January 1960.
2. Stations closed before 1900 are not shown.
3. To assist clarity, most colliery, industrial and goods-only branches are not shown.
4. Only the longer tunnels are shown.

© R.A.Smith, February 2019. No. 2004, v2.3.

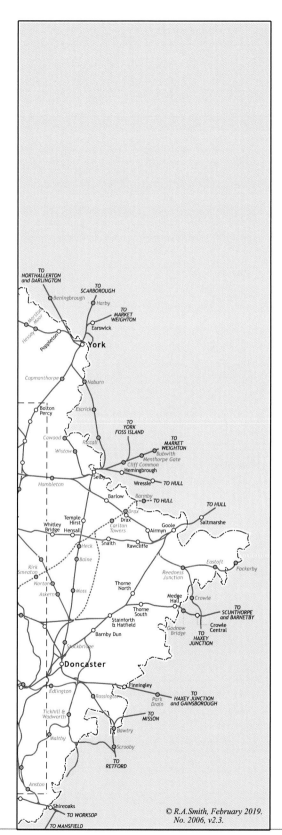

In conditions typical of the Settle & Carlisle Railway, Stanier Class 5 4-6-0 No.45027 tackles the last few yards to Ais Gill summit with a train of vans on 12th August 1967. The vehicles illustrated above are the sturdy four wheel short-wheelbase vans, often described by railwaymen as 'Vanfits', which were restricted to a maximum speed of 45mph due their notorious instability at high speeds. Once an everyday sight across the British Railways network, they have long been consigned to the history books. The photographer had seen a picture taken from this viewpoint reproduced in a railway magazine and was determined to capture a similar one to this on colour film. Much to the chagrin of the gallery of photographers positioned behind him he had to make a mad dash to avoid being in their picture. *Derek Huntriss*

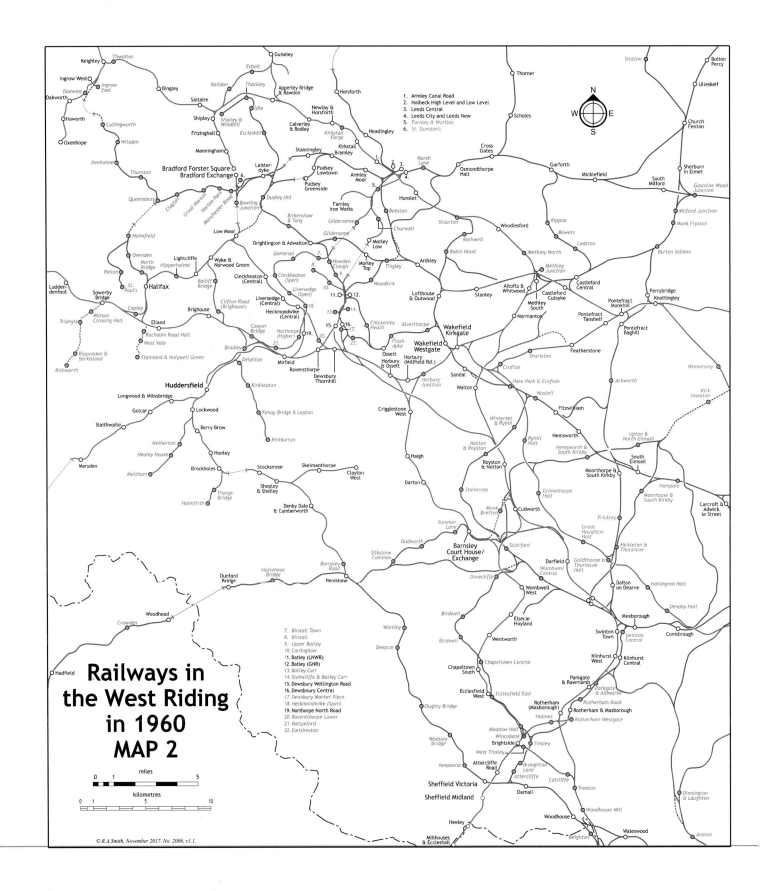

The snow covered Wild Boar Fell makes an impressive backdrop to this picture of Stanier Class 8F 2-8-0 No.48375 as it nears Ais Gill summit on 31st March 1967. Set in the midst of bleak and mountainous country, this land was once occupied by Norse invaders about a thousand years ago who left their mark for posterity in many of the region's place names. Gill is the old Norse name for a small ravine containing a fast running stream, scores of these abounding in this area cutting deep clefts into these North Pennine Fells. Ais is also a derivation from the old Norse and could be a settler's name such as Asulf or from Eikis, the word for Oak. The summit of the line is some 1 1/2 miles south of the actual Ais Gill which is crossed by means of Ais Gill viaduct. This train has climbed the 14 miles of 1 in 100 from Ormside Viaduct before it reaches the easier grades to Blea Moor Tunnel and the descent to Settle Junction. At Ais Gill summit the railway is in a shallow cutting but this poses no obstacle to the splendid views in all directions. Wild Boar Fell rises to 2,324ft above sea level and dominates the whole area with its scars and screes, ending in the Nab giving the mountain its familiar classic shape. *Gerald Dixon*

On 27th September 1963 a Fowler Class 4F 0-6-0 approaches Shotlock Hill Tunnel between Ais Gill and Garsdale with an up freight. The tunnel goes through Shortclick Hill suggesting something has been lost in translation! Shotlock Hill Tunnel is only 108 yards in length and the hillside is shallow here, the tunnel appearing to be superfluous where a cutting would surely have sufficed. *David Mitchell*

Taken on 10th August 1966 this view of Garsdale station is looking towards the south west. In the foreground can be seen the remains of the bay platform for trains to Northallerton. The North Eastern line from Northallerton to Hawes closed to passenger traffic in April 1954. Goods traffic ceased between Redmire and Hawes in 1964, and the track was subsequently lifted. Goods traffic from Northallerton to Redmire ceased in 1982. Passenger traffic between Garsdale and Hawes was withdrawn on 16th March 1959, followed by goods traffic in April 1964, after which the track was lifted. However, the Wensleydale Railway was formed in 1990 with the object of reopening the line as a Heritage Railway. It has so far succeeded in restoring service over the 16 miles between Leeming Bar and Redmire, and hopes eventually to reopen the remaining 24 miles. At the back of the station the water tower can be seen. It was almost identical to that at Settle, and was where the local community used to hold dances in happier times. It, and six others along the S&C, was demolished in the 1970s after steam had ended its days. The Settle tower is now the only survivor. *Tommy Tomalin*

The 'Bobby' hangs out of the box at Dent station as BR Class 9F 2-10-0 No 92016 heads north with an early morning freight on 14th July 1967.
It stood on the down side of the line, south of the station. It had about twenty levers and controlled eight signals: down distant, home and starter, up outer distant, inner distant, home and starter, and one dwarf shunting signal, out of the down siding. Dent box had points for an up siding, two outlets from a down siding, and a trailing crossover between the up and down lines with a slip into the cattle dock. The two outlets from the down siding allowed goods wagons to be detached from down freights and run round to be propelled into the dock. Detachment to the dock from an up train was simply through the crossover and slip. Apart from wagons intended for Dent, there were occasional 'hot boxes' to put off: wagons with overheated axle boxes noticed by a preceding signal box, and detached for attention by the carriage and wagon fitter from Skipton. If the damage to a loaded wagon was beyond repair, a platelayer willing to tranship the ten tons of coal over the end of the damaged wagon into another wagon had to be found. Emptied, the C&W fitter would patch up the axle box for the wagon to go to Skipton for new wheels. Dent Station Box was manned from 6.00am Monday to 6.00am Sunday and was switched out during Sundays. There were three regular signalmen, working early, late and night shifts in turn. *Derek Huntriss*

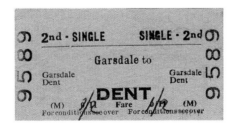

After emerging from the 2,629yds long Blea Moor Tunnel a pair of Stanier 8F 2-8-0s are seen crossing the ten-span Dent Head viaduct hauling new pre-fabricated 60ft panels of concrete sleepers in August 1967. The lonely outpost of Blea Moor is set high in the Pennine wilderness traversed by the Settle-Carlisle line of the former Midland Railway. When it is not swept by driving rain or lost in rolling mist it presents an inspiring scene. As the train soars above Dent Dale it will pass the closed signal box at Dent Head and cross Arten Gill viaduct before reaching Dent. The locos on this train had taken water at the Blea Moor water station, its two columns being fed by the plentiful supply draining from Whernside. Drivers of engines wishing to take water at Blea Moor would usually whistle, one long and three short, when passing Horton or Dent. This wasn't the intention of being heard at Blea Moor; the message being telephoned on ahead so that if the demands of traffic required the train could be put into the loop. Occasionally trains would be put into the loop involuntarily, to be held for a train of some superior classification to pass by, or possibly for crew to be exchanged with those of an opposite-bound train. *Derek Huntriss*

An unidentified Jubilee Class 4-6-0 heads across Ribblehead viaduct with a northbound passenger train on 25th August 1962. Taking five years to construct, the 440yd, 24 arch viaduct had every 6th arch strengthened and built to larger dimensions using the logic that if one arch should ever fall only five would follow. At its height, construction of the Settle-Carlisle railway line employed 7,000 men. Nearly 1,000 of these worked at Ribblehead on the major engineering tasks of building the Ribblehead viaduct and Blea Moor Tunnel. The area is bleak and isolated and so accommodation had to be specially built to house this army of workers. Construction camps, or shanty towns as they are popularly called, grew up between 1870 and 1875 and their remains can still be seen as low earthworks and flat building platforms. Most of the workers lived in prefabricated single-storey wooden terraces, but the Batty Wife Hole settlement also included more substantial buildings such as shops, public houses, a school, post office and library as well as a small isolation hospital built during a smallpox epidemic. Closer to Ribblehead viaduct lay the engineering camp of Sebastopol with its suburb, Belgravia. Sebastopol included a large brickworks as well as terraced lodging houses and an engine house with a sunken inspection pit. Remains of the brickworks can still be seen. *David Mitchell*

The rail train illustrated on page 10 is seen again, this time crossing Ribblehead viaduct, the photographer having taken advantage of the water stop at Blea Moor to catch it at Dent Head. Some two years earlier in the early morning of December 1965, gale-force winds had blown seven new cars off a goods train crossing the viaduct. They were being transported on flat wagons from Luton to Scotland, two being reported to have landed in the valley below. Other trains were safely halted by an observant signalman, but the inclement conditions made it difficult for a time to begin clearing the line as it was unsafe to stand upright on the viaduct; a locomotive and snow plough were brought in to tackle the debris along one track. The first train to pass, an overnight sleeper service, arrived at St. Pancras more than six hours late. *Derek Huntriss*

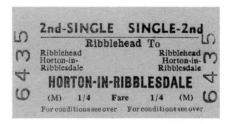

With snow still clinging to the peak of Pen-y-Ghent, Stanier Class 8F 2-8-0 No.48469 is captured near Horton-in-Ribblesdale with a Brindle Heath to Carlisle freight on 31st May 1967. Built at Swindon Works in March 1945 as No.8469 this loco was renumbered 48469 during w/e 15th October 1949. At the time of the photo it was allocated to Bolton mpd from where it was withdrawn from traffic on 16th December 1967, being cut up on site. Pen-y-Ghent is one of the mountains known collectively as the Yorkshire Three Peaks. The station and the village of Horton-in-Ribblesdale is located 850 feet above sea level and is approximately 6 miles north of Settle. The line from Settle Junction to Blea Moor is often called the 'Long Drag' and has a ruling gradient of 1 in 100 except for a short section of level track north of Helwith Bridge where the line crosses the site of an old glacial lake. There were two sets of sidings at Helwith Bridge serving both the Ribblesdale Lime Works and the Helwith Bridge Granite Company. These were taken out of use in September 1969 after which Helwith Bridge signal box was closed. *Gerald Dixon*

During the summer of 1967 Jubilee 4-6-os were booked to work the 6.40am Birmingham to Glasgow which they took over at Leeds City and worked as far as Carlisle. Here No.45562 *Alberta* crosses the infant river Ribble near Stainforth on 12 August. Departing from Leeds at 10.17am this train was a regular Jubilee turn throughout that summer until Saturday 26th August, the last day of its operation. The excellent external condition of the locomotive was the result of overnight cleaning by members of the Master Neverers Association enthusiast group who spent many Friday nights at Leeds Holbeck MPD polishing the pride back into the remaining members of this well-known class. *Derek Huntriss*

BR Standard Class 9F 2-10-0 No.92004 drifts downhill through Settle station with a train of anhydrite from Long Meg Sidings to Widnes on 23rd March 1967. The station was designed by Midland Railway architect, John Holloway Sanders, and was opened with the line on 1st May 1876. Originally named Settle New to distinguish it from the nearby station on a different route, which was renamed Settle Old at the same time. Settle New was renamed Settle on 1st July 1879, by which time Settle Old had become Giggleswick. Goods facilities were withdrawn from the station in 1970. *Gerald Dixon*

Stanier Class 5 4-6-0 No.44854 passes the long-closed station at Settle Junction with a freight from the Morecambe line. It was situated immediately to the south of the junction between the Midland Railway's 'Little' North Western and Settle-Carlisle lines, some 39 3/4 miles northwest of Leeds. It was opened five months after the main line to Carlisle to serve as an 'exchange station' with the older route to Morecambe. However, the expected traffic failed to materialise and after just one year of operation, it was closed on 1st November 1877. Its remote location, 1 3/4 miles south of Settle and 2 miles north of Long Preston undoubtedly contributed to its early demise, as potential travellers had the choice of three alternative stations (Settle, Giggleswick or Long Preston) that were all more conveniently sited for their respective communities. Little trace of the station remains today, although the station house survived in private ownership until well after nationalisation of the railways in 1948, finally succumbing to demolition in the late 1960s. *David Mitchell*

BR Standard Class 4 4-6-0s Nos.75051 and 75039 work the 12.40pm Heysham Moss to Tees Yard freight as they pass Clapham, Yorkshire, at 1.56pm on 22nd April 1965. The line diverging to the right behind the leading loco is that to Sedbergh and Ingleton which eventually joined the West Coast main line at Low Gill. This branch was closed to passenger traffic on 1 February 1954 and completely in July 1966 although regular goods traffic had ended some months earlier. Lifting of the track followed in April 1967. A sharp curve (with a permanent 35 mph speed restriction) marks the site of the former junction, immediately west of Clapham station. It had ceased to handle goods traffic in 1968, when the remaining sidings were taken out of use and dismantled and the station signal box closed. *Derrick Codling*

This Easter 1966 picture sees Stanier Class 5 4-6-0 No.44926 just east of Clapham station with a Leeds to Morecambe train. The original Midland Railway main line headed west from Skipton, where it met the Leeds and Bradford Railway, and headed west towards Lancaster. Whilst the stations at Giggleswick, Long Preston, Bell Busk and Gargrave were ornate, the stations at the country junctions of Clapham and Wennington were more skimpy constructions. Following the opening of the line through Ingleton and Sedbergh (which was owned by the London & North Western north of Ingleton) the Midland developed an interest in the growing Anglo-Scottish traffic. It was the intransigence of the LNWR that led to the opening of the region's last great extension on 1st May 1876 - the Settle-Carlisle line. *David Mitchell*

This undated image depicts Stanier Class 5 4-6-0 No.45209 preparing to enter the sidings at Giggleswick on the 'Little' North Western, where the station, like those at Bell Busk and Gargrave, was distinguished by pictureseque half-timbered buidings. *Derek Phillips*

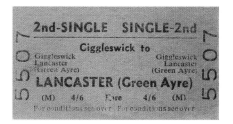

The somewhat dilapidated 'Little' North Western station at Long Preston is seen here on 7th May 1967. It was opened in July 1849, the North Western Railway timetable for January to June 1860 showing four trains per day from Leeds to Lancaster from where connections could be made to Carlisle and Scotland. *Tommy Tomalin*

Stanier Class 5 4-6-0 No.44727 is the standby loco in this view looking west at Hellifield on 7th May 1967. Today Hellifield is one of the least attractive of the Dales villages but before 1830 it was a small rural hamlet eeking out an existence based on cotton weaving and agriculture. Initially it was served by a small Midland Railway station about 1/2 mile south of the present one. This was built as cheaply as possible, contractors being given the basic layout and accommodation requirements and the materials to be used. In an effort to reduce costs the building was constructed of wood and plaster to a villa design with mock tudor styling. When the Lancashire & Yorkshire Railway opened their line from Chatburn a new joint station was brought into use. Substantial terraced houses were subsequently built for their workers by both companies. Midland Terrace consisting of some 40 three-bedroom dwellings whilst Lancashire & Yorkshire Terrace had eight houses. By 1895 the junction complex had been operating for some 15 years and out of Hellifield's 104 houses, 65 were occupied by railway families. Hellifield's dependence on the railway continued through LMS days and well into British Railways but by the late 1950s a general decline had set in. *Tommy Tomalin*

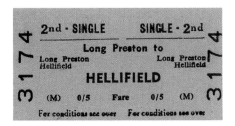

This August 1967 picture sees an unidentified Stanier Class 5 4-6-0 striking out from Hellifield towards Skipton. Not only have steam locomotives disappeared but the wagons, telegraph poles and signals are now all part of railway history. *Derek Huntriss*

This stunning winter scene taken in February 1966 sees BR Standard Class 4 4-6-0 No.75051 with a SO Skipton to Lancaster and Morecambe stopping train as it heads along the straight away from the closed station at Bell Busk which is out of view around the corner. The station at Bell Busk had a somewhat unusual claim to fame in that it was used as a shooting location for the 1951 feature film, Another Man's Poison. The film's main star, noted American actress Bette Davis was apparently so impressed by it (according to reports in the local press) that she enquired if the station was for sale. It is not known whether her interest was genuine or not, but no formal purchase offer was made and so it remained in use until 1959, when it was closed by the British Transport Commission. Although more than 100 local objections were lodged to the proposed closure, the local Transport Users' Committee accepted the British Railways arguments that the station was unviable and it was duly closed to passengers on 4th May 1959. *David Mitchell*

Stanier 8F 2-8-0 No.48746 has received an impromtu cleaning from a summer shower as it heads a rail train between Gargrave and Hellifield in August 1967. It is working a train of bogie wagons conveying concrete-sleeper track from Dewsnap (Guide Bridge) to Carlisle. The new track was being used for the West Coast Main Line and was laid near Gretna the following day. Powerful, versatile and reliable, William Stanier's Class 8F was the most advanced freight locomotive built before Nationalisation. Unglamorous perhaps, but this no-nonsense workhorse became one of the last surviving steam classes on British Railways. In 1939, the design was chosen for military service overseas, more than 200 being built on government account by North British Locomotive Co and Beyer-Peacock between 1940 and 1942. In addition to these another 51 LMS engines of this class were given air pumps together with other minor modifications before being requisitioned by the WD. *Derek Huntriss*

At Skipton the MR waited until 30th July 1849 before work began to extend the line towards Ribblesdale as a joint venture by the Midland Railway and 'Little' North Western Railway, it going only as far north as a junction with the Lancaster & Carlisle at Ingleton. However, this wasn't an equal partnership, the Midland Railway was looking for its own route culminating with the Settle & Carlisle. Here in August 1967 we see super power for an empty stock working as a BR Standard Class 9F 2-10-0 pilots a Stanier Class 5 with its eight-coach train including several former LMS vehicles. *Derek Huntriss*

Stanier 8F 2-8-0 No.48537 has passed under the 'gallows' signal at Skipton station with a westbound freight in September 1965. On 30th April 1876, Skipton station was relocated 10 chains northwest of its original location. By then, both the Leeds & Bradford & North Western railways had been absorbed by the Midland Railway. The new station coincided with the opening of the Midland's Settle-Carlisle Line, which put Skipton on the London St Pancras to Glasgow main line. The new station had four platforms and cost over £15,000, compared with the original station's cost of £2,300. Platform 1 was a bay platform at the Bradford end, adjacent to the station building along with through platform 2, while platforms 3 and 4 formed an island platform. On 1st October 1888 platforms 5 and 6 were added to serve the Skipton to Ilkley Line, which opened that day. These platforms were at a slightly higher level on a rising gradient, as the new line ran southwest of the existing line and then crossed over it by bridge eastwards. These platforms were also later used by the Yorkshire Dales Railway, a short branch to Grassington open to passengers between 1902 and 1930. Passenger services to Ilkley ceased on 22nd March 1965 after which platforms 5 and 6 were closed to passengers and their access subway was bricked off. However, the line through platform 5 is still in use as a single-track freight line to Swinden Quarry via the former Yorkshire Dales line. The track through platform 6 has been lifted. *David Mitchell*

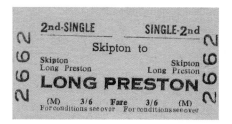

Barnoldswick railway station was the only station on the Midland Railway's 1 mile 64 chains long Barnoldswick Branch in the West Riding of Yorkshire. The line left the Leeds and Bradford Extension Railway at Barnoldswick Junction, 55 chains from Earby railway station. The line through the junction was on a 20 chain radius after which it converged to a single track and ran in a straight but undulating line to Barnoldswick. The passenger train that ran back and forth between Barnoldswick and Earby was known locally as the 'Barlick Spud' or 'Spudroaster'. The real reason for the name is lost in time, but the two versions that were commonly recited are that the original branch locomotive was so small it looked like a portable potato roaster used by a local vendor or that the journey time was the same as that taken to roast a potato in the locomotive's smokebox. Here BR Standard Class 2 2-6-2T No.84015 awaits departure from Barnoldswick for Earby in November 1964. From September 1956 the service had been reduced to just one train in and two out per day. This later changed to just one in and one out, plus a single mid-day goods train, a pattern that was maintained until the last passenger train ran on Saturday 26th September 1965. *Richard Greenwood MBE*

Tender-cab fitted Class 4F 0-6-0 No.44468 is captured performing shunting activities at Grassington on 26th March 1964. At that time the daily freight from Skipton to Swinden lime works was in the hands of a Skipton 4F but was latterly worked by BR Standard Class 4MT 4-6-os from either Skipton, Rose Grove or Carnforth MPDs. These workings kept alive the old days on a country branch line where a photographer could get away from civilisation for an hour or two. The line was at its most pleasant in a morning with the sun rising catching those characteristically subtle tones on the Pennines which surround the line. There was a small country pub between Rylstone and Skipton with its excellent food and pleasant company or the old signal box at Grassington which was later turned into a rescue post. Whilst these things were common to all country branch lines they were were more pertinent here because they were the last. *David Mitchell*

Late evening sun catches Fowler Class 4F 0-6-0 No.44220 as it prepares to depart from Grassington on Sunday 29th July 1962 with a ten-coach return ramblers' excursion to Blackburn. Leaving at 7.40pm this loco took the train as far as Skipton where it was replaced by Stanier Class 5 4-6-0 No.45187 for the rest of the journey. These excursions were to cease with the closure of the line beyond the quarry at Swinden in August 1969. Diverging from the Skipton to Ilkley railway at Embsay Junction the Grassington Branch had only one intermediate station at Rylstone. The village of Rylstone became famous when members of the Women's Institute were the inspiration for the film 'Calendar Girls'. Filming took place in the summer of 2002 in and around the village of Kettlewell in North Yorkshire, some ten miles away. The penultimate shot of Chris and Annie walking down a street was filmed in Turville. *John Langford*

Photographed in the last months of steam operation over the Grassington Branch BR Standard Class 4 4-6-0 No.75027 crosses the level crossing at Cracoe on 25th May 1968. Latterly worked by a Rose Grove engine (7.25am from Skipton) it returned from the quarry an hour or so later. Normally conveying hoppers to Bamber Bridge, it was on several occasions diverted to Appleby. The usual locos were Nos.75019 and 75027 (seen here) which were kept in immaculate condition by enthusiasts. *Gerald Dixon*

Previously depicted on page 24, tender-cab fitted Class 4F 0-6-0 No.44468, which was seen shunting at Grassington, is now seen returning to Skipton Rylstone level crossing. On the left is a signal having Midland Railway origins whilst that on the right is LNWR. The Beeching Report, published in 1963, proposed closure of the entire railway network in Wharfedale. 22nd March 1965 was the last day of passenger services over the Arthington to Burley and Ilkley to Skipton lines. A few months later they were closed to all traffic and track lifting soon commenced. The exception was the the branch between Skipton and the quarry at Embsay which was used for a further year before being cut back to the junction with the Grassington Branch which still serves Swinden Quarry. *David Mitchell*

This picture taken near Rylstone level crossing sees BR Standard Class 4 4-6-0 No.75019 as it works tender-first with a rake of an empty wagons for Swinden quarry on 31st May 1968. At Grassington the former Midland Railway station site has now been built upon, the housing estate being known as Piece Fields. The reason for tender-first working was that there were no turning facilities at Swinden. Angular, handsome, efficient and built too late, the BR Standards worked until the last breath of British main line steam. At the beginning of their last full year in service, 1967, there were only 46 of the 80 BR Standard Class 4 4-6-0s left in service, all LMR engines apart from a small Southern allocation. *Gerald Dixon*

Situated at Rylstone on the southern fringe of the Yorkshire Dales, Swinden Quarry is some seven miles north of Skipton and three miles from the picturesque Wharfedale village of Grassington. The area is rich in high-quality reef limestone and quarrying has been taking place at Swinden since the the latter part of the nineteenth century. It was in 1902 that the Midland Railway built one of its last lines, that from Embsay Junction (near Skipton) to Grassington running right past the quarry. Since the closure of the section beyond Swinden to Grassington quarry production has been the sole source of traffic on the line. Notwithstanding this the line today is one of the most intensively worked and profitable single track freight lines - or if one goes by the latest OS maps, 'mineral lines' in the country. Here BR Standard Class 4 4-6-0 No.75019 blasts away from Swinden lime works on 1st June 1968. *Gerald Dixon*

Having taken the token for the Grassington Branch from the signalman at Embsay Junction near Skipton, tender-first BR Standard Class 4 No.75019 heads for the quarry at Swinden on 31st May 1968. The Grassington Branch was one of the last lines to open in the county and whilst nominally independent until the Grouping in 1923, it was operated by the Midland Railway. Whilst passenger services over the line were withdrawn in September 1930, the line continued to enjoy sizeable business from excursion traffic from day trippers from the West Riding and Lancashire coming to the Dales. *Gerald Dixon*

An elevated view of the station at Bolton Abbey on the former Midland Railway branch from Skipton to Ilkley taken on 29th July 1962. WIth a set of LNER stock in the siding there is little evidence of goods traffic in the yard but the line lasted for passenger traffic until 22nd March 1965. The line through Wharfedale opened in several stages - the North Eastern's section from Otley to Arthington opened on 1st February 1865 and the Midland's line from Ilkley to Apperley Junction and the joint section to Otley on 1st August 1865. 4th December 1876 saw the opening of the section from Shipley to Guiseley with the line from Ilkley finally reaching Skipton on 1 October 1888 giving the Midland a second through route from Skipton to the industrial West Riding. *John Langford*

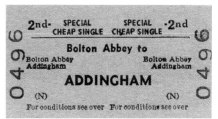

The original Ingrow West station building seen here before BR closure on 28th May 1960 was badly vandalised between the time the Keighley to Oxenhope branch line closed on 1st January 1962 and its re-opening as the Keighley & Worth Valley Railway in 1968. The new Company could not use the station and all that could be done was to keep it tidy and use it as an unstaffed request stop. The title 'West' was added in BR days, Ingrow GN becoming Ingrow East. At this point the line passes under the Halifax road by means of Ingrow Tunnel, 150yd in length, beyond which a short siding served Ingrow and Grove Mills. The line then crosses the River Worth for the second time and continues to climb to the diminuitive station at Damems, two miles from Keighley, and is said to have been the smallest station on the Midland system. The gradient then steepens to 1 in 60 for nearly a mile to Oakworth. *John Langford*

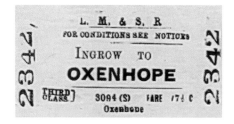

Ingrow West station on 28th May 1960 looking down the Worth Valley towards Keighley. Former Midland Railway fencing and a distant signal are in evidence, plus local transport. Ingrow East station on the former GNR Keighley to Queensbury line which closed to passengers on 23rd May 1955 was just beyond the trees on the right of the picture. At this time, and until July 1961, goods traffic continued at Keighley South GNR station, served by a trip working from the Midland station, reversing near Ingrow East, but the track had been lifted through the long tunnel south of Ingrow. *John Langford*

Clean Ivatt Class 2 2-6-2T No.41273 works the Worth Valley Branch on 28th May 1960 and is depicted at Haworth station with its LMS three-coach push-pull set. The lack of passengers clearly shows the increasingly strained financial circumstances of branch lines such as this and was why so many of them disappeared. *John Langford*

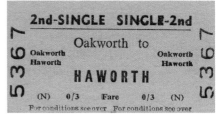

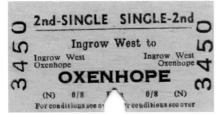

On 28th May 1960 Ivatt 2-6-2T No.41273 has reached the terminus of the branch at Oxenhope. On Mondays-Fridays in the 1950s there was no train out of Oxenhope between 8.20am and 1.45pm. This enabled the branch goods to do its shunting and the motor-train had a fill-in turn from Keighley to Bradford and back. On more than one occasion the Johnson tank failed at Bradford, and Manningham had to supply a standby engine until Skipton could send down a replacement motor-fitted engine. The Johnson 0-4-4 tanks were replaced in May 1952 when new Ivatt Class 2 2-6-2 tanks were allocated to Skipton. *John Langford*

Stanier Class 5 4-6-0 No.45273 coasts round the curve through Keighley station with a Bradford Forster Square to Heysham parcels working in July 1967. Situated on the western fringe of the industrial West Riding the town of Keighley is at the confluence of the rivers Aire and Worth. The pattern of communications in this part of Airedale was a product of the last Ice Age when it was buried under a vast glacier. Steep melt water channels which later became swift-flowing streams became much sought-after sites for woollen mills and the valleys of the River Worth and Bridgehouse Beck were no exception. Despite having ideal locations the mill owners still had problems in transporting coal and raw materials to their mills, and finished cloth to the markets was relatively expensive. The coming of the Leeds & Bradford Extension Railway to Keighley on 16th March 1847 eased the problem but didn't help the mill owners along the Worth Valley. After many years of difficult negotiations with the Midland Railway the Worth Valley branch to Oxenhope was finally opened on Saturday 13th April 1867. *Derek Penney*

This September 1966 view taken near Crossflatts between Keighley and Bingley sees Stanier 8F 2-8-0 No.48332 with a rake of 16 ton mineral wagons as it heads east towards Bingley. The route from Shipley to Skipton was never quadrupled throughout but from Bingley to Thwaites there were goods lines on the outside of the two passenger lines. That in the foreground can be seen to have had little use and was removed a year later. A wooden halt was opened at Crossflatts in 1892 on a site where the Midland Railway always held out against building a station. However that company did yield to pressure for passenger facilities at Thwaites but found the response very disappointing. Today there is no visible evidence of that station which closed in 1909 after a life of only 17 years. *Derek Penney*

A view looking east at the same location as the previous picture sees Class 4 2-6-0 No.43135 as it crosses the River Aire with a westbound mixed freight, again in September 1966. The Leeds & Bradford Railway opened the Leeds & Bradford Extension Railway from Shipley to Keighley on 16th March 1847. Bingley station opened on the first day, and remained the only intermediate station until Saltaire was built in 1856. The original station, near the Three Rise Locks, was originally of wood, but the Midland Railway (which had absorbed the L&BR in 1851) closed the old station and opened the current station on 24th July 1892. The bog north of Bingley station was a headache to the railway builders. It is recorded in the Bradford Observer of 8th March 1847 that 'no fewer than 100,000 cubic yards of solid earth and stone have been poured into this insatiable maw of a bog.' The bog has also claimed some of Bingley Grammar School's buildings and the sinking may have given rise to an urban legend about a locomotive and wagons being swallowed up by the bog although no evidence can be found to attest to this. *Derek Penney*

This undated picture sees Fairburn 2-6-4T No.42138 during its stop at Shipley with a train from Bradford Forster Square to Leeds. The present station was built at some time between 1883 and 1892, nestling between the western (Bradford-Skipton) and eastern (Leeds-Bradford) arms of the triangle. It was designed by the Midland Railway's architect Charles Trubshaw. Platform 3 (on the Bradford-Leeds arm) was lengthened in 1990, to serve full-length InterCity trains. The northern (Leeds-Skipton) arm of the triangle is distant from the main station and had no platforms until May 1979. Before then, trains on the Leeds-Shipley-Skipton run had to come through the station to the Bradford branch and reverse. *David Mitchell*

Also undated is this picture of Britannia Pacific No.70053 *Moray Firth* as it approaches Shipley station with a westbound evening parcels train. Until the Beeching Axe closures of 1965, the next stations from Shipley were Saltaire on the Airedale line to the west, Baildon on the Wharfedale line to the North, Apperley Bridge in the east towards Leeds, and Frizinghall in the south towards Bradford. Baildon station closed on 5th January 1953, re-opening again on 27th January 1957 before final closure came on 29th April 1957. *David Mitchell*

BR Standard Class 9F 2-10-0 No.92056 is in charge of the 1.30pm Leeds to Carlisle freight as it passes the signal box at Shipley Bingley Junction on 2nd September 1967. As a professional architect, the photographer's keen eye brings into sharp relief the detail in the terraced properties commonly seen in the West Riding. The signal box was to see a second life once made redundant when it was transported by train from its original location to the Keighley & Worth Valley Railway. The KWVR used its own breakdown crane to manoeuvre the signal box into place in Keighley station. This historic signal box was brought back into use in 2015 - 23 years after it was installed. *Gerald Dixon*

Thompson Class B1 4-6-0 No.61016 is depicted in the yard at Thornton on the old GN Queensbury-Keighley line with a train on 20th August 1964. On several occasions after World War II, Thornton won the best kept station award. Goods services ceased in 1965 after which the line was lifted. *Gavin Morrison*

Ivatt Class 2 2-6-2T No.41282 is propelling an Officer's Inspection train at Queensbury station in October 1962. At this triangular station it is standing in what was the Bradford to Halifax platform. The Queensbury to Keighley section was closed to all regular traffic in May 1956, but the line shot into prominence at the beginning of 1958 when Class A3 Pacific No.60081 *Shotover* and two 1,000hp English Electric Class 20 diesels appeared for tests in the 1,534 yards long Lees Moor Tunnel. *David Mitchell*

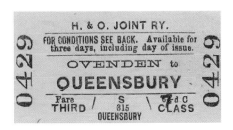

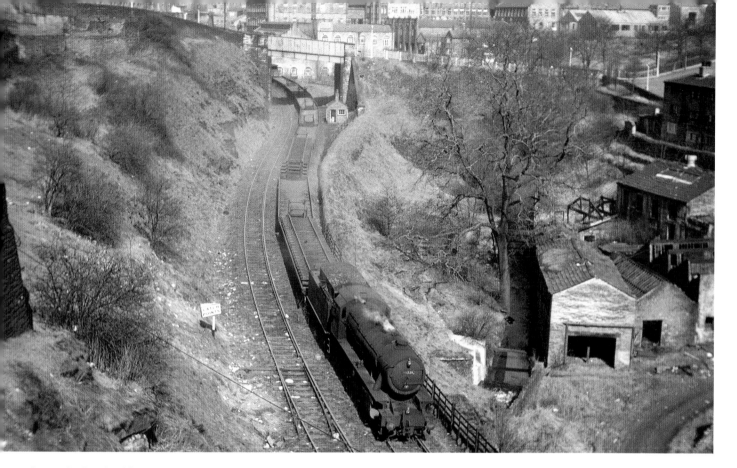

e northern suburbs of Halifax, WD 2-8-0 No.90329 approaches Lee Bank tunnel on the former Great Northern Railway line between Ovenden and ax North Bridge with a track lifting train on 30th March 1963. The Queensbury lines which had cost aroung £1 million to build probably never fulfilled expectations and further threats to their existence came in the form of municipal tramways in both Halifax and Bradford. Locomotives used for these were of mainly GNR origin, latterly Class N1 0-6-2Ts based at Bradford, although there was a small sub-shed at Ingrow, part of which survives. The ensbury Triangle routes are now but a distant memory but what surviving structures that remain are a tribute to the Victorian ethos that railways could and serve most parts of the kingdom. *David Mitchell*

Between duties hauling tracklifting trains WD 2-8-0 No.90412 is seen on 22nd March 1963 at the site of the former Halifax North Bridge station. *David Mitchell*

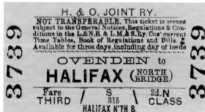

With Summit East Box visible on the left of this picture WD 2-8-0 No.90725 is about to enter Summit Tunnel between Todmorden and Littleborough with the midday Healey Mills to Arpley freight c1962. Running from Manchester to Normanton and engineered by George Stephenson the line was the first to cross the Pennines. Taking almost five years to complete, the final section between Hebden Bridge and Littleborough was opened in March 1841 after the construction of three viaducts and seven tunnels in the space of 10 miles. Summit Tunnel at 1 mile 1125 yards passed under the Pennine watershed, took three years to complete and claimed nine lives. For a very brief time it had claim to being the world's longest tunnel. *Richard Greenwood MBE*

3rd · SINGLE   SINGLE · 3rd

WALSDEN TO

Walsden   Walsden
Littleborough   Littleborough

LITTLEBOROUGH

(M)   0/8   Fare   0/8   (M)

For conditions see over   For conditions see over

5845   5845

On 6th August 1961, the last day of stopping passenger trains, Fowler Crab 2-6-0 No.42863 is captured leaving Walsden near Todmorden. This station, which was opened in 1845 by the Manchester & Leeds Railway, predecessor of the Lancashire & Yorkshire Railway, was situated between the level crossing and the north portal of Winterbutlee Tunnel. The level crossing visible next to the second coach was abolished a few years later and is today the site of a new station opened in September 1990. *Richard Greenwood MBE*

Patricroft MPD's Jubilee Class 4-6-0 No.45558 *Manitoba* is seen departing from the east end of Todmorden station with an SSuO Llandudno to Bradford train on 4th August 1962. The station at Todmorden was famous for its prize-winning garden displays and cast concrete BR lion and wheel emblems. One of these was situated on the Leeds platform and the other at Hall Royd and painted in the correct colours were the work of a permanent way man called O'Neil. Also on the Leeds platform the displays included a fountain, with a fish tank on the Manchester platform. The viaduct visible between the signals passed over Burnley Road in the centre of Todmorden and the town's bus station. *Richard Greenwood MBE*

This undated picture was taken from the bridge at Hall Royd Junction, a long time popular vantage point for photographers, and depicts Stanier Class 5 4-6-0 No.45200 as it comes off the line from Copy Pit with an eastbound train of empty loose-coupled wagons. Between the tunnels on the Calder Valley line between Todmorden and Hebden Bridge frequent glimpses can be had of the Calder Valley's most prominent landmark, the stone obelisk that sits on the 1,300ft Stoodley Pike. *Richard Greenwood MBE*

Mons Mill, Todmorden and the Pennines form a backdrop to this picture of Britannia Class Pacific No.70013 *Oliver Cromwell* as it begins the climb from Stansfield Hall Junction to Copy Pit summit on 21st July 1968. This tour organised by the Roch Valley Railway Society was to travel between Manchester and Southport by four different routes. No.70013 took over from Stanier Class 5 4-6-0 No.44888 at the Southport avoiding curve and proceeded to Wigan Wallgate via Meols Cop. Taking the train back to Manchester Victoria via Bolton it has taken the Calder Valley route to Todmorden where it begins the ascent to Copy Pit summit and finally arrived back at Southport Chapel Street. *Derek Huntriss*

Rose Grove MPD's Stanier Class 8F 2-8-0 No.48247 heads a coal train from Healey Mills to Rose Grove over Lydgate Viaduct, Todmorden on 24th February 1968 with classmate No.48257 providing assistance at the rear. The depot at Rose Grove provided motive power for through traffic between Preston and Healey Mills over Copy Pit as well as serving a stream of coal trains between Burnley and Burn Naze (Fleetwood). The supply of banking engines to Todmorden and some express freight workings to the Manchester area kept about 25 Class 8Fs and a number of Class 5s fairly busy. Both of these locomotives were built by the North British Locomotive Co for the War Department in 1940 being numbered WD301/21 but allocated LMS numbers 8227/47 respectively. They were shipped to Persia in September 1941 becoming 70301/95. In September 1949 they were bought by BR taking the numbers 48247/57 respectively. *Derek Huntriss*

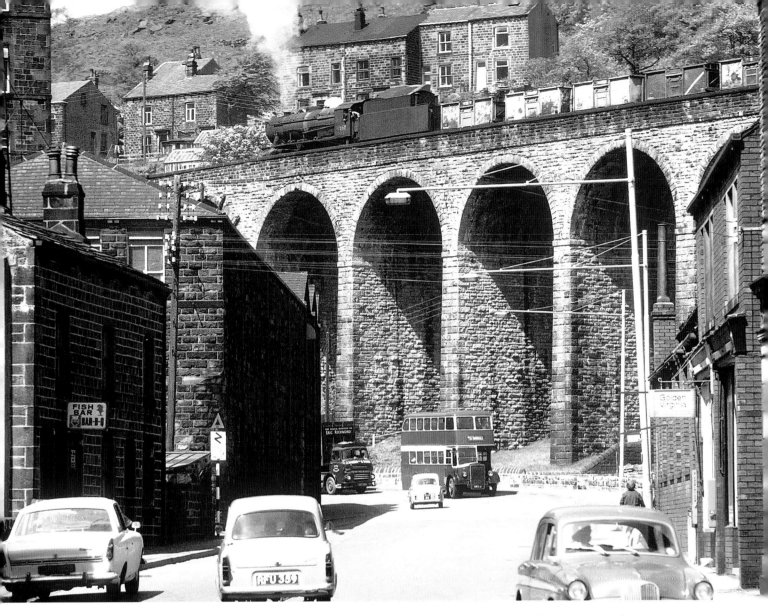

Above: Built for the War Department by Vulcan Foundry in 1944 (Works No.4983) 2-8-0 No. 90611 climbs towards Copy Pit Summit over Cornholme viaduct with a coal train for Lancashire on 28th May 1966. Approaching the photographer is a Todmorden Joint Omnibus Committee's greeen and cream liveried vehicle. Renowned for their spotless condition inside and out they were partly run by the railway. Like Halifax, the LMS was a partner with the TJOC. The once-familiar Leyland double-deckers with the LMS crest on their sides had to be a low bridge variety, otherwise they would not fit into the town's bus garage. To achieve their low profile the top deck seats were all to one side with the gangway in a well along the other. Passengers downstairs had to watch their heads as the gangway well protruded below the lower deck ceiling. *Gerald Dixon*

Opposite: Attached at Stansfield Hall Junction in Todmorden for the ascent to Copy Pit summit Stanier 8F 2-8-0 No.48448 shoves a heavy coal train up the tortuous 1 in 65 over Lydgate viaduct in Todmorden. Instead of using a traditional front three-quarter view the photographer has incorporated his architectural skills to capture the train framed by mill buildings typical of the West Riding. *Gerald Dixon*

Another Todmorden Joint Omnibus Committee vehicle heading towards Hebden Bridge is captured in this picture as Stanier 8F 2-8-0 No.48448 exits Horsfall Tunnel with a westbound goods train on 28th May 1966. In this part of the Calder Valley, rail, road and canal run parallel. In the foreground is the Rochdale Canal which apart from a short profitable section in Manchester linking the Bridgewater and Ashton Canals, was closed in 1952 when an act of parliament was obtained to ban public navigation. The last complete journey had taken place in 1937 and by the mid 1960s the remainder was almost unusable. Construction of the M62 motorway in the late 1960s took no account of the canal, cutting it in two. After massive restoration projects the restored sections joined up with the section in Manchester below the Ashton Canal junction, which had never been closed, and on 1st July 2002 the canal was open for navigation along its entire length. *Gerald Dixon*

Running alongside the main A646, Halifax to Burnley road, Stanier 8F 2-8-0 No.48448 heads a loaded coal train across Lobb Mill viaduct between Todmorden and Hebden Bridge on 28th May 1966. *Gerald Dixon*

Right: A 2-6-4T has crossed over to the down platform at Hebden Bridge station to unload parcels from a Bradford Exchange to Rochdale working. Miraculously Hebden Bridge station escaped the years of rationalisation when most stations were stripped of everything but the bare essentials. With platform canopies, parcels lift and L&Y signs all intact, it was fully restored in the 1970s and won several awards. The goods facilities were withdrawn from 2nd May 1966, the goods yard becoming the station car park. *Derek Phillips*

Below: This superb picture taken at Mytholmroyd looking towards Hebden Bridge shows WD 2-8-0s passing with coal trains. The up train carries loaded wagons for Lancashire and the returning empties are bound for the Yorkshire coalfields. Right of centre on the distant hillside the profile of St. Thomas the Apostle church at Heptonstall can be seen.
Richard Greenwood MBE

47

Opposite: The photographer has once again used his architect's eye to capture BR Standard Class 5 No.73053 against the industrial backdrop of Sowerby Bridge on 12th August 1967 as it works the 1.35pm SO service from Scarborough to Manchester. *Gerald Dixon*

Right: Ex-LYR 0-6-0 No.52515 rests outside Sowerby Bridge MPD on 2nd September 1962. Together with No.52121 it was still active as Greetland and Hebden Bridge pilots. Of the other two members of the class at that depot No.52461 had been plundered for spares and No.52413 was intact but awaiting a new lubricator. Later that year on 29th September No.52515 was used to pilot Class 4F 0-6-0 No.44408 on a railway enthusiasts excursion from Sowerby Bridge and Halifax to Doncaster and Darlington. *Ray Cook/Neville Simms Collection*

Below: This panoramic view of Sowerby Bridge taken on 20th August 1966 sees Jubilee 4-6-0 No.45565 *Victoria* as it heads the 1.25pm SO train from Blackpool to Leeds. *Gerald Dixon*

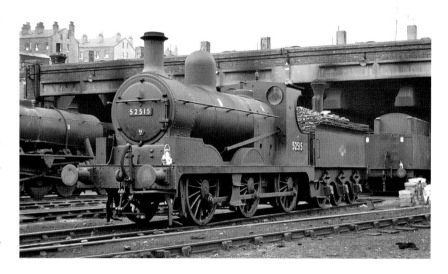

Looking east from above the tunnel over the site of the former L&Y station at Elland on 2nd June 1966 after the buildings had been demolished, Ivatt Class 4 2-6-0 No.43098 passes light engine. The modern signal box seen to the right of the site of the platform had replaced Elland East and West boxes together with Waterhouse Siding box in 1958. Some years earlier in 1956 goods facilities had included a covered two-face dock, an 8 ton yard crane and a large wool and grain warehouse, the station closing on 10th September 1962. *Gerald Dixon*

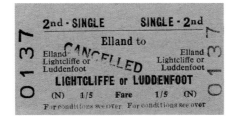

Class O4 2-8-0 No.63588 waits in the yard at Brighouse on 24th May 1960 with a freight about to head up the Calder Valley, probably going as far as Mytholmroyd Yard. Note the WD 2-8-0 behind the first train. At this time it was quite usual to have coal trains queuing up behind each other in yards and loops. *Gavin Morrison*

A pair of Stanier Class 5 4-6-0s are seen on Whit Monday 1966 as they double-head the Newcastle-Red Bank vans through Brighouse. The northern editions of a number of national newspapers were printed in Manchester and, largely unseen, the loaded trains travelled through the night, but the daytime return of the empty vans attracted much attention. By virtue of their exceptional length they were regularly double-headed. Throughout the week the train returned from York and ran via Leeds City, Morley and Thornhill LNWR Junction where it transferred to the ex-L&YR Calder Valley main line to continue through Brighouse, Hebden Bridge, Rochdale, Castleton East Junction, Newton Heath, and Cheetham Hill Junction terminating at Red Bank Sidings. *David Mitchell*

2nd - SINGLE	SINGLE - 2nd
2448	Brighouse for Rastrick to	2448
	Brighouse for Rastrick Manchester (Victoria)	Brighouse for Rastrick Manchester (Victoria)
	MANCHESTER (VICTORIA)	
	via Todmorden	
	(N) 9/6 Fare 9/6 (N)	
	For conditions see over	For conditions see over

Situated roughly mid-way between Brighouse and Mirfield the junction at Heaton Lodge was one of the most complex 'rural' junctions on the LMS. Here Fowler 2-6-4T No. 42406 is seen with a Wakefield-Huddersfield local in July 1957. At that time, a day at the 'Lodge' would guarantee local 'Spotters' a profusion of express passenger, freight and local workings. In the left background can be seen the track-bed of the former LNW Leeds New Line, later known as the Spen Valley Line, which enabled LNW trains to run from Huddersfield to Leeds via Heckmondwike and Cleckheaton, without the need to run over L&Y track. *David Kelso*

Manchester Longsight MPD's Royal Scot 4-6-0 No.46143 *The South Staffordshire Regiment* is seen at Heaton Lodge Junction in July 1958 as it works a Liverpool-Newcastle train. Having left Huddersfield it is joining the L&Y line and will leave the Calder Valley main line after passing Mirfield at Thornhill LNW Junction and travel to Leeds via Heckmondwyke.The first coach is a rarity and is Derby built Lot 1654. It was a 57ft corridor brake first, one of 25 built at Derby in 1927. In the 1933 re-numbering they became 5011 to 5035 and one, 5034, ended up as part of the Royal Train. *David Kelso*

The photographer captured this excellent silhouette of Jubilee 4-6-0 No.45565 *Victoria* as it works a SO Blackpool-Leeds train past Heaton Lodge Junction on 6th August 1966. By the 1930s the levels of traffic converging at Heaton Lodge led the LMS to introduce a 'speed signalling' installation in 1932, which not only indicated to drivers which route to be taken but also determined the speed to be held over the junction. Unique in Britain this system was based on an American practice and lasted until the early 1960s when the new Healey Mills marshalling yard was being developed. *Gerald Dixon*

With Mirfield MPD visible in the distance through the haze Stanier 8F 2-8-0 No.48321 approaches Heaton Lodge Junction with a westbound freight on 3rd May 1968. The ex-L&YR main line, with its regular coal trains, remained one of the most important steam-hauled main lines until the end of steam operation on the North Eastern Region. This section of the L&YR main line was to lose its regular passenger services in 1970, leaving Brighouse as one of the largest towns in the West Riding without a passenger service although Brighouse station subsequently reopened. The trackbed of the former Leeds New lines heading towards Battyeford can clearly be seen in the background. *Gerald Dixon*

An unidentified WD 2-8-0 is seen passing Mirfield MPD with a loaded coal train in May 1966. The loco is passing the depot's 'coal hole' which remained in use until the end of steam. Alongside the coal hole are a pair of colour light signal posts, the down inner homes of Mirfield's No.1 box, itself just visible in the distance by the junction of the Newtown Branch. These signals dated from July 1932, when a section of the Calder Valley main line saw the first full application in this country of the new 'speed' signalling principles which covered a total of 2 3/4 miles. *David Mitchell*

This view of Mirfield MPD taken some three years earlier on 28th July 1963 sees Fowler 2-6-0 'Crab' 2-6-0 No.42923 outside the shed. Mirfield is better known today as the birthplace of Sir Patrick Stewart OBE, who played Picard in *Star Trek: The Next Generation*. Built in 1885 the shed was designed to accomodate thirty-two engines which in the early years included a variety of 0-6-0s, 0-6-2Ts and saddle tanks. In LMS days its eight roads could hold 28-30 engines under cover. The depot's allocation eventually rose to over fifty locomotives, many of them 0-6-0s which were engaged on coal workings. After a number of 'final reprieves' the shed eventually closed in April 1967. The original date chosen for closure was 2nd January that year, but various delays were encountered before Mirfield crews could be found satisfactory accommodation at Healey Mills.
Gerald Dixon

With the cooling towers of Thornhill power station in the backbround, Stanier Class 5 4-6-0 No.44928 heads the SO 10.48am Filey to Manchester service through the Calder Valley on 6th August 1966. At this point the former L&Y and LNWR lines run parallel with the line to Leeds diverging to the left. One of the smallest coal-fired power stations in the region, Thornhill was rail-served for many years. *David Mitchell*

2nd · SINGLE   SINGLE · 2nd

Thornhill (for Dewsbury) to

Thornhill
(for Dewsbury)
Mirfield

Thornhill
(for Dewsbury)
Mirfield

MIRFIELD

(N)   0/6   Fare   0/6   (N)

For conditions see over   For conditions see over

WD 2-8-0 No.90076 prepares to go on shed at Normanton MPD on 4th July 1967. Prior to its brief one month allocation to Normanton MPD it had spent much of the previous eight years allocated to Wakefield MPD. It was despatched to West Hartlepool MPD in September from where it was withdrawn in September 1967. Its final journey was to Arnott Young's scrapyard, Dinsdale, for cutting up. *Peter Fitton*

2nd · SINGLE   SINGLE · 2nd
Normanton to
Normanton   Normanton
Castleford (Central)   Castleford (Central)
CASTLEFORD (CENTRAL)
(N)   1/2   Fare   1/2   (N)
For conditions see over   For conditions see over

One of the last duties to be undertaken by a Jubilee Class 4-6-0 in BR ownership was performed by No.45562 *Alberta* on 28th October 1967 when it was rostered to haul a Manchester Railway Society / Severn Valley Railway Society special. During the early hours of the morning the author, together with other members of the MNA enthusiast group, prepared the loco to 'Royal Train' condition prior to the tour. During the course of preparation the yellow warning stripes on the cabsides were painted over but whilst grabbing a couple of hours sleep in the back of a car they had been reinstated. During that year the eight surviving Jubilees had soldiered on in the Leeds, Bradford and Wakefield areas, No.45562 being the last member of the class to be withdrawn. *Derek Huntriss*

Later on 28th October 1967, only weeks before the depot at Normanton closed, snowplough-fitted Stanier Class 5 No.44902 is captured next to the ash plant. Immediately to the left of the loco can be seen the narrow gauge rails that carried the ash tubs; one being visible adjacent to the cab. The original station at Normanton was opened by the North Midland Railway (NMR) on 30th June 1840 on their main line towards Leeds, creating an interchange station between the North Midland Railway (NMR), the York and North Midland Railway (Y&NMR) and the Manchester and Leeds Railway (M&LR) and became a station on the first East Coast main line. Through services on the Leeds & Manchester Railway from Manchester to Normanton began on 1st March 1841, the first section of the M&L from Manchester (Oldham Road) to Littleborough having opened on 4th July 1839 with a daily service of seven trains each way. The completed railway was heavily engineered and the aptly named Summit Tunnel at 1 mile 1,125 yards was the first tunnel of such a length anywhere in the world. The Leeds & Manchester lines crossed a 51-mile stretch across the Pennines and at the time Normanton had the world's longest railway station platform at a quarter of a mile long. The station was, for the next ten years or so, the most important in England, employing over 700 people who looked after the station's 700,000 passengers a year. *Dick Manton*

This superb picture captures BR Standard Class 9F 2-10-0 No.92082 as it passes Normanton Station South signalbox with a Leeds Neville Hill to Stanlow empty oil tank working on 28th October 1967. It was standard practice with hazardous loads to have a barrier wagon behind the loco as can be seen here. In January 1850 the Joint Committee responsible for the working of the station at Normanton decided to provide a shed together with sidings and a turntable for the use of the various companies using the station. A building authorised in 1886 is believed to have been the roundhouse which was shared by Midland and North Eastern Railway's engines whilst the Lancashire & Yorkshire Railway's shed was the straight shed, which remained in use until the depot closed. From 1st October 1938 the LMS assumed full control of the shed and from that date the LNER paid a rental for their engines actually stationed there. On 1st January 1957 Normanton (together with a number of other sheds in the West Riding) was transferred from the London Midland Region to the North Eastern Region and recoded from 20D to 55E. By this time the former NER Class J71s allocated to Normanton had been scrapped and were replaced by two Class J72 0-6-0Ts Nos.68681 and 68701 which were joined by No.68726 in February 1958. The North Eastern Railway's long association with Normanton was continued when the four Q6 Class 0-8-0s which were at Neville Hill were transferred on 12th June 1966. They remained until 2nd October 1966 when they were reallocated to Tyne Dock with the shed closing completely on 1st January 1968. *Dick Manton*

Britannia Pacific No.70038 *Robin Hood* drifts down the 1 in 175 gradient over Saddleworth viaduct with a returning Stephenson Locomotive Society tour from York on 2nd July 1967. Below the viaduct to the left, the canal can be seen crossing the River Tame. The viaduct and canal lock are fantastic examples of Victorian engineering and are Grade II listed. *Jim Bodfish/KRM*

Diggle station was situated where the four tracks of the former LNWR line from Manchester to Huddersfield emerged from the western portals of the Standedge tunnels. Here BR Standard Class 5 4-6-0s Nos.73050 and 73069 pass through the somewhat derelict station with the SVRS / MRTS 1Z77 North West Tour on 27th April 1968. The platforms and overbridge can be seen with the booking office next to the bridge. *S. Wolstenholme/KRM*

ROUTE OVER STANDEDGE

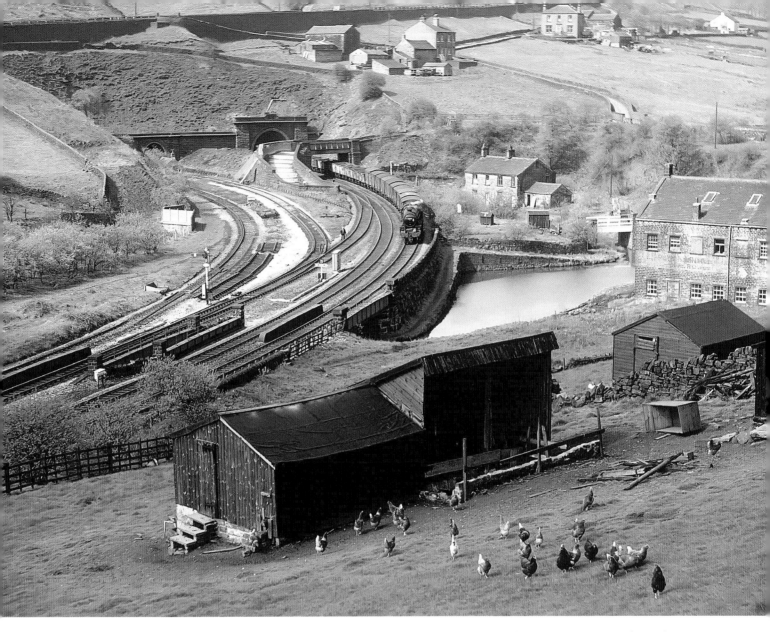

At 3 miles 66yd, Standedge Tunnel is one of the longest in Britain. This bucolic scene at the eastern end of the tunnel was captured on 3rd May 1968 as Stanier Class 5 No.45046 begins the descent of mainly 1 in 105 to Huddersfield. From left to right are the 1871 'Nelson' tunnel which is behind the embankment, the 1849 'Nicholson' and the 1894 double line bore. Today only the 1894 rail tunnel is in use for rail traffic. In 1966, the 1848 single-track rail tunnel was closed followed by the 1871 single-track tunnel in 1970 although today the 1848 and 1871 tunnels are used by maintenance personnel for access. *Gerald Dixon*

0944 | 2nd-SINGLE   SINGLE-2nd | 0944
Marsden to
Marsden
Slaithwaite
Marsden
Slaithwaite
SLAITHWAITE
(N)   1/0   Fare   1/0   (N)
For conditions see over   For conditions see over

Above the mills and chimneys of Slaithwaite on the climb to Standege Tunnel, Stanier Class 5 No.45242 heads a westbound freight over the imposing viaduct which dominates the town on 7th May 1966. The following month the two single-line tunnels achieved fame when preliminary tests were carried out under the auspices of the Channel Tunnel Co with a diesel-hauled test train, in order to ascertain measurements of air pressure and wind speeds to assist in determining the size of clearances required for 'Chunnel' operations. For this purpose 31 ventilating shafts were sealed off. With rationalistaion and the re-routing of some services over the Calder Valley route the two single-line bores were taken out of use from October 30th 1966, the newer double line bore then carrying all traffic over this route through the Pennines. *Gerald Dixon*

2nd-SINGLE   SINGLE-2nd

Slaithwaite to

Slaithwaite
Marsden, etc.

Slaithwaite
Longwood, etc.

LONGWOOD or MARSDEN

(N)   1/0   Fare   1/0   (N)

For conditions see over   For conditions see over

3501

3501

Devoid of front numberplate and in poor external condition BR Standard Class 9F 2-10-0 No.92132 passes through the station at Slaithwaite with a Leeds Neville Hill-Stanlow empty oil tank working on 7th May 1966. This duty took the train via Goosehill Junction, Healey Mills and Standedge. For many years this locomotive was allocated to Wellingborough MPD, ending its days at Carlisle Kingmoor from where it was withdrawn in October 1967. *Gerald Dixon*

In this picture the photographer has captured the essence of a West Riding mill town as Stanier Class 5 No.45235 crosses the viaduct with the 12.30pm SO Leeds-Manchester at Longwood, near Huddersfield, on 5th August 1967. In 1879, the London & North Western Railway received new powers to double their lines in the Huddersfield area and work on the immense task started in 1880. Evidence of the widening of the Longwood Viaduct, which was completed in 1884, may easily be seen in the walls and arched roof where there is a noticeable difference in construction styles. *Gerald Dixon*

Britannia Pacific No.70038 *Robin Hood* passes the signal box at Linthwaite on 2nd July 1967 with the return leg of an SLS railtour which ran from Birmingham (New Street) to York where there was an official visit to York MPD. Steam operations at York had finished the previous month although some stored locos were observed in the yard. It was reported that the return run over Standedge was very poor, the brakes coming on at least two or three times, presumably through lack of vacuum. With the exception of No.70013 *Oliver Cromwell* which was retained for working special trains in the final year of steam operations on British Railways, all of the remaining Britannia Pacifics were withdrawn at the end of 1967. Built in 1951 and originally allocated to the Eastern Region No.70013 was the last BR steam locomotive to be overhauled in BR workshops emerging from Crewe Works on 2nd February 1967. The quadruple track seen in this picture had been extended from Huddersfield to Golcar in 1887 and to Slaithwaite in 1890 before reaching Marsden on 1st November 1891. *Peter Fitton*

The photographer has once again captured the raw atmosphere of the West Riding with mill chimneys and millstone grit terraced houses. Here an unidentified Class 9F BR Standard 2-10-0 heads a tank train over Longwood viaduct near Huddersfield on the climb to Standedge Tunnel on 18th August 1967. *Gerald Dixon*

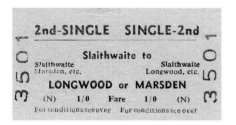

An air of neglect pervades this picture taken at Longwood station as Stanier 8F 2-8-0 No.48612 drifts downhill from Marsden on 19th April 1968. Longwood, Golcar and Slaithwaite stations were closed on 7th October 1968 when the Huddersfield-Manchester local service was practically withdrawn. Marsden was left with a few token stops by through trains and a FO rush hour service was retained between Greenfield and Manchester. There had been a threat to close Morley, Batley and Ravensthorpe stations but this was lifted in 1969, the stopping service between Huddersfield and Leeds being reduced to a minimum. *Gerald Dixon*

Tom Greaves, who was the Divisional Motive Power Superintendent West Riding in 1967, ensured that three Jubilee Class 4-6-0s were available in good order for the summer relie workings. Without doubt steam enthusiasts the time surely owe Tom and his shed staff Holbeck, led by Ted Geeson, a great debt of gratitude for providing the spectacle of thes fine locomotives hard at work in the Pennine Here No.45593 *Kolhapur* powers away from Huddersfield with the 11.25am Newcastle-Llandudno on 8th July 1967. *Gerald Dixon*

Fowler 'Crab' 2-6-0 No.42817 passes throug station at Huddersfield with a westbound fr on 15th May 1964. *Gerald Dixon*

Situated in a suburb of Huddersfield on the Penistone line, Lockwood viaduct crosses over the River Holme and having 34 arches measures 476 yards in length. The viaduct was designed by noted civil engineer John Hawkshaw for the Huddersfield & Sheffield Junction Railway, which was formed to build a line between Huddersfield and a junction on the existing Sheffield, Ashton-under-Lyne & Manchester Railway near to the station at Penistone. The master mason was Job Hirst, son of Joshua 'Red Jos' Hirst of Kirkheaton, who later built railway viaducts in India. The foundation stone was laid in April 1846 by the wife of the contractor, John Shaw (of Messrs. G. Miller & Co.). The 972,000 cubic feet of sandstone for the viaduct was quarried from the railway cutting at Berry Brow. Here Jubilee Class 4-6-0 No.45647 *Sturdee* traverses the viaduct on 2nd July 1966 with the SO working through train from Leeds to Poole. Today this fine view is obscured by tree growth. *Gerald Dixon*

Having traversed the Meltham branch, BR Standard Class 4 2-6-4T No.80044 catches the late evening light as it returns to Meltham Branch Junction with 'The Pennine Rose Rail Tour' on 2nd May 1959. This tour organised by the Railway Enthusiasts Club of Farnborough ran from Stalybridge to Huddersfield and back terminating at Oldham Road Goods in Manchester. In the left background is David Brown Tractors' Meltham Mills site with the spire of St. James church in Meltham Mills on the right. *David Kelso*

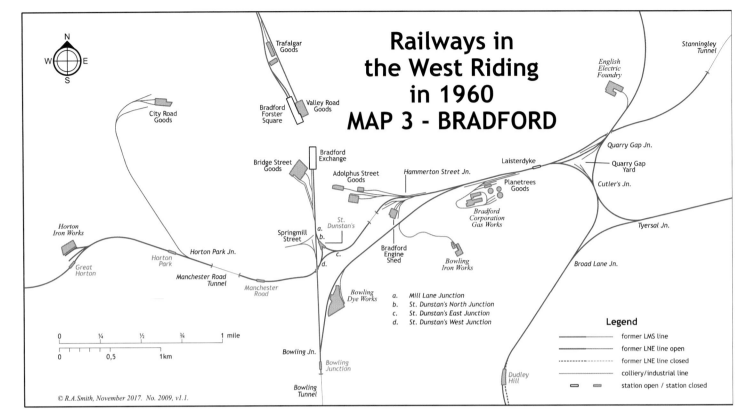

Railways in the West Riding in 1960
MAP 3 - BRADFORD

Trafalgar Goods

City Road Goods

Bradford Forster Square

Valley Road Goods

Stanningley Tunnel

English Electric Foundry

Quarry Gap Jn.

Bradford Exchange

Bridge Street Goods

Adolphus Street Goods

Hammerton Street Jn.

Laisterdyke

Quarry Gap Yard

Cutler's Jn.

Planetrees Goods

Bradford Corporation Gas Works

Tyersal Jn.

Horton Iron Works

St. Dunstan's

Springmill Street

a.
b.

c.

d.

Bradford Engine Shed

Bowling Iron Works

Broad Lane Jn.

Horton Park Jn.

Horton Park

Great Horton

Manchester Road Tunnel

Manchester Road

Bowling Dye Works

Bowling Iron Works

a.   Mill Lane Junction
b.   St. Dunstan's North Junction
c.   St. Dunstan's East Junction
d.   St. Dunstan's West Junction

Bowling Jn.

Bowling Junction

Bowling Tunnel

Dudley Hill

Legend

————	former LMS line
————	former LNE line open
-------	former LNE line closed
————	colliery/industrial line
▭ ▭	station open / station closed

0   ¼   ½   ¾   1 mile

0   0,5   1km

© R.A.Smith, November 2017. No. 2009, v1.1.

Jubilee 4-6-0 No.45593 *Kolhapur* (playfully named Batman) is seen rounding the curve after passing Shipley Bradford Junction with a returning holiday excursion for Bradford Forster Square in July 1966. *Derek Penney*

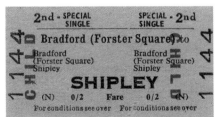

Stanier Class 5 4-6-0 No.44916 is seen passing Manningham Junction (Bradford) signal box as it heads the 3.18pm Bradford to Heysham parcels on 7th June 1967. Manningham Junction signal box controlled traffic on the main line and into the loco depot with Manningham station and motive power depot behind the photographer. In the background can be seen Valley Road power station. Bradford possessed the country's first municipally-owned power station - situated on Bolton Road - in 1887 and when this became too small, a large facility was opened at Valley Road in 1896/7. This closed in 1976 and was largeley demolished in 1978. In the late 1950s the shed at Manningham was home to about a dozen different steam types including a trio of Compound 4-4-0s whose duties included the Bradford Forster Square-Morecambe 'Residential' which carried wool magnates home to the Lancashire resort. *Peter Fitton*

2nd · SINGLE   SINGLE · 2nd
Frizinghall to
Frizinghall   Frizinghall
Manningham, etc.   Manningham, etc.
MANNINGHAM or SHIPLEY
(N) 0/2 Fare 0/2 (N)
For conditions see over For conditions see over

4794

A variety of ex-LMS motive power is seen around the roundhouse turntable inside Bradford Manningham MPD in this superbly atmospheric picture taken on 28th July 1963. Locos include Ivatt Class 4 2-6-0s Nos.43074 and 43030 together with Fairburn 2-6-4Ts Nos. 42138,42093 and 42189. The depot at Manningham was opened in 1872 and replaced an older shed which had been closer to the terminus at Forster Square. Its purpose was to service the route which had been opened by the Leeds and Bradford Railway (later Midland Railway) with motive power for a range of local and long-distance trains. Apart from MR trains the station at Forster Square also played host to a through service to Harrogate which was operated by the North Eastern Railway (later LNER) over the Otley & Ilkley Joint line. *Gerald Dixon*

A Stanier Class 5 4-6-0 is seen leaving the depot at Bradford Manningham on Whit Monday 1966 with the station clearly visible behind the loco. Opening in 17th March 1868 Manningham was the first stop out of Bradford on the Midland Railway (originally the Leeds and Bradford Railway), built in 1846. From 1872, an extensive network of sidings and sheds was developed to the north of the station. Station closure under the Beeching Axe came on 22nd March 1965. *David Mitchell*

LMS Fairburn 2-6-4T No.42093 is using the freight lines behind the station at Manningham as it takes empty stock into Bradford Forster Square on 30th May 1966. In the summer of 1957 Manningham was served by nine trains to Skipton, eight to Leeds City, three to Ilkley and one each to Morecambe, Carlisle, and Skipton via Ilkley. The station closed on 22nd March 1965 when the local service to Leeds was withdrawn. In the 1950s, and up to closure in 1965, the Bradford Railway Circle used a hut on the platform at Manningham station for its meetings. No.42093 had been allocated to Manningham since April 1957 before it was transferred to Normanton shed in April 1967 from where it was withdrawn from traffic in October that year. *David Mitchell*

This panoramic view looking north at Bradford Forster Square station was taken on 24th June 1967. One of the last remaining Jubilee Class 4-6-0s, No.45562 *Alberta*, waits to leave light engine. Forster Square was an important terminus, sending passenger trains to London, the Midlands, the West Country and the North. In the summer of 1957, in addition to local trains to Leeds City, Ilkley and Skipton, there were four trains a day to St. Pancras, three to Morecambe, two to Bristol and one each to Bournemouth, Newcastle, Scarborough, Paignton, Hull, Sheffield, Derby, Garsdale, Carlisle and Heysham Harbour. The extensive marshalling yards appear to be busy in this picture with parcels traffic continuing to flourish after the station had lost its main line passenger trains, thanks to orders despatched by Bradford mail order houses Grattan and Empire Stores. Most of the platforms were given over to parcels trains which left every night for destinations all over the country. By the late 1970s the traffic declined as haulage was switched to road transport, the final death knell coming in 1980 when BR closed its Collection and Delivery parcels service. *Peter Fitton*

With Forster Square's Valley Road goods complex on the left Stanier Class 5 4-6-0 No.44916 is seen leaving with the 3.18pm parcels working to Heysham on 8th August 1967. The carriage sidings at Forster Square survived well into the 1980s, as did much of the station layout, and were used for storing withdrawn electric units from London's Great Eastern suburban lines during their journey to the scrapyard. In the early 1960s the station throat was full of MIdland character with Midland Railway lower-quadrant signals and gas lamps. These were replaced when signalling was modernised between 1961 and 1964. In the background the tower of Bradford Cathedral can be seen. *Peter Fitton*

1st- SINGLE   SINGLE - 1st
Bradford (Forster Square) to
Bradford   Bradford
(Forster Square)   (Forster Square)
London (St. Panc.)   London (St. Panc.)
LONDON (ST. PANCRAS)
via Leeds, Normanton, Sheffield & Leicester
For alternative routes see book of routes
(N)   78/6   Fare   78/6   (N)
For conditions see over   For conditions see over

Stanier Class 5 4-6-0 No.45428 is seen under the arched roof at Bradford Exchange station with what was the penultimate steam-hauled passenger train to operate on the North Eastern Region of British Railways, the 2.20pm to Leeds on 1st October 1967. Later that day it was Fairburn 2-6-4T No.42152 that had the honour of working the final steam-hauled train to Leeds. The story of Bradford Exchange (originally Bradford L&Y) began in 1850 when it became the first terminus to open on the south side of the city. Completed by the L&Y it was initially served only by trains which had travelled from Mirfield via the Spen Valley route. This line brought passengers through the delights of Cleckheaton, Low Moor and St. Dunstans and concluded with a two mile descent at a gradient of 1 in 50. By comparison the GN route with its terminus at Adolphus Street had conveniently avoided the difficult civil engineering problems of getting rails into the city, but faced passengers with a long uphill toil from the town centre.
David Rodgers

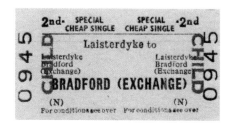

Another Stanier Class 5 4-6-0, this time ex-works No.44807, is captured in March 1967 as it begins the climb out of Exchange station. The station was completely rebuilt on the same site in 1880 with ten terminating platforms and two arched roofs. Constructed of wrought iron, these rested at the outer sides on plain stone walls and classical corinthian style columns down the middle. Glass covered the middle half and timber (inside) / slate (outside) covered the outer quarters of each span. The four end screens were glazed in a fan pattern with decorative timber outer edging. The dimensions were a length of 450 feet, a width of 100 feet for each arch and a height of 80 feet, track to apex. The railway station never had a formal frontage; instead, passengers entered by an opening in the northwest side. The original Lancashire & Yorkshire Railway terminus in Bradford was situated at Adolphus street, but the facilities were inadequate and inconveniently sited. The station was closed to passengers in 1867 and the line was extended into Exchange station situated closer to the city centre near to the wool exchange, after which it was named. The new station was opened by the joint efforts of the Lancashire and Yorkshire Railway and the Great Northern Railway on 9th May 1850. In 1867, the Leeds, Bradford and Halifax Junction Railway, which had previously used Bradford Adolphus Street, built a link to the tracks into Exchange station to join the two existing companies; Adolphus Street station was then closed to passengers. *Derek Penney*

Above: This superb action shot captures Fairburn 2-6-4T No.42251 as it heads away from St. Dunstan's under Bridge Street bridge with the Bradford portion of a King's Cross express on 25th September 1967. It was the condition of this bridge that was one factor in the decision to close the original Exchange station and construct the new station allied to a bus station south of the bridge. This was, however, the swan-song of West Riding steam as visits to the nearby sheds Hammerton Street (ex-Great Northern), Low Moor (ex-Lancashire & Yorkshire), and Manningham (ex-Midland) testified. *Gerald Dixon*

Opposite: Fairburn 2-6-4Ts Nos.42066 and 42073 blast up the 1 in 50 out of Bradford Exchange with the 9.40am excursion to Bridlington on Whit Monday, 25th May 1967. The 2-6-4Ts would have worked the train as far as Leeds City. No.42066 survived a futher four months at Low Moor MPD before withdrawal and No.42073 was transferred to Normanton MPD from where it was withdrawn. Periods in store at Mirfield and Carnforth followed before it was reprieved and is now one of two class members preserved on the Lakeside & Haverthwaite Railway. *Peter Fitton*

Fairburn 2-6-4T No.42196 is seen rounding the curve at St. Dunstan's Junction on 16th September 1966 with the 9.0am Bradford Exchange to King's Cross. This train worked directly to Wakefield Westgate where it would be coupled to the portion from Leeds. On summer Saturdays in particular, a visitor to Exchange would be treated to a parade of steam-hauled trains which, even as late as 1966, included Stanier and Fairburn 2-6-4Ts, Stanier Class 5s, B1s, Jubilees and Ivatt Class 2 2-6-0s. Steam still virtually monopolised the shuttle connections to Wakefield Westgate, which utilised the Copley Hill curve to the GN main line at Wortley South Junction. *Peter Fitton*

WD 2-8-0 No.90711 has a brake van in tow as it returns from Thornton on 21st October 1963 and takes the Laisterdyke curve at St. Dunstan's. A platform at the closed station at St. Dunstan's which closed in December 1952, is visible on the left. The track layout at St. Dunstans was unusual, in that trains branched off eastwards at Mill Lane Junction and passed through St.Dunstans. Then a triangular junction allowed through running to Leeds, or by curling back round under the Bradford Exchange to Manchester line, trains could continue to Queensbury. There was a third side to the triangle which allowed through running from Queensbury to Leeds but was used almost exclusively by goods trains and had no passenger platforms. *David Mitchell*

The parting of the L&Y and GN routes out of Bradford Exchange was controlled by St. Dunstan's signal box. Behind the box are the lines to Halifax with Stanier 2-6-4T No.42616 passing the site of St. Dunstan's station on the line to Leeds. It is working the 10.5am Bradford portion of the 'Devonian' on 2nd June 1967. No.42616 had only recently been reallocated from Birkenhead MPD where it had seen use on Birkenhead to Chester services. The station at St. Dunstan's had closed on 15th September 1952. *Peter Fitton*

Stanier Class 5 4-6-0 No.45273 drifts slowly downhill at Bowling Junction as No.42073 is seen again, this time on 8th July 1967 working the 9.6am Bradford Exchange to Poole with the line to Laisterdyke diverging to the right. *Gerald Dixon*

Having passed through the station at Laisterdyke, Fairburn 2-6-4T No.42073 has the through coaches of an express for KIng's Cross on 13th June 1967. The station was closed to passengers on 4th July 1966, on the same day as the line to Ardsley, and the platforms were subsequently demolished. *Peter Fitton*

Stanier 2-6-4T No.42616 passes the overhanging signal box at Laisterdyke West as it heads the 7.45am Bradford Exchange to Yarmouth on 22nd July 1967. Some three years earlier on 10th November 1964 while pulling an Ardsley to Bradford Adolphus Street freight, Class 4 2-6-0 No.43072 got out of control on the steep incline between Laisterdyke and Hammerton St. No.43072 ran through the goods yard at Adolphus Street colliding with the buffers and then the engine and tender smashed through a wall and dropped 40ft into Dryden Street. The remains of No.43072 were promptly sold to a local scrap merchant, Butlers Ironworks, which undertook to cut up the locomotive and carry it away. This operation took six days. *Gerald Dixon*

BR Standard Class 5 4-6-0 No.73141 climbs the 1 in 50 incline towards Bowling Junction with the summer SO 8.20am Bradford Exchange to Bridlington via Halifax on 1st July 1967. The white steam beyond the bridge is from a former LMS 2-6-4T which is providing some welcome rear-end assistance. Then based at Patricroft MPD No.73141 was one of 30 members of the class built at Derby with Caprotti valve gear, the remaining 142 members of the class were constructed with the more conventional Walschaerts valve gear. Less than 12 years old No.73141 succumbed to the cutters' torch on 28th February 1968 at Cashmore's yard in Newport. *Peter Fitton*

Emerging from Crewe Works in December 1947 the now-preserved Stanier Class 5 4-6-0 No.44767 was constructed with Stephenson link motion and a double chimney, the latter being replaced with a single chimney in 1953. Spending its early years at former L&Y sheds it arrived at Bank Hall MPD in February 1950, moving a little further north to Southport in March 1962 before being despatched to Carlisle Kingmoor in November 1964. Whilst allocated to Bank Hall it was frequently diagrammed on trans-Pennine services. Here it is seen leaving Halifax on 28th August 1961 as it works a combined Bradford Exchange/ Leeds Central to Liverpool Exchange train. The portions on these trains were normally pieced together, or separated, at Low Moor, otherwise the manoeuvre took place at Halifax. The Leeds portion had travelled over former GN metals to Bowling Junction on the outskirts of Bradford. *Gavin Morrison*

2nd-SINGLE		SINGLE-2nd
9753	Sowerby Bridge to	9753
	Sowerby Bridge Halifax or Mytholmroyd	Sowerby Bridge Halifax or Mytholmroyd
	HALIFAX or MYTHOLMROYD	
	(N) 1/0 Fare 1/0 (N) For conditions see over For conditions see over	

This undated view sees former L&Y 0-6-0 No.52400 on station pilot duties at Halifax station. The Class 27 locomotives were designed by John Aspinall, 484 being built between 1889 and 1918 at Horwich Works. It was the standard goods engine used by the Lancashire & Yorkshire Railway. Aspinall opted for a two-cylinder format with a non-superheated round top boiler. David Joy's configuration of valve gear was employed. By the time Aspinall became general manager of the L&YR on 1st July 1899 more than 400 of the simple but powerful engines had been built. More were built under his successors, Henry Hoy and George Hughes, albeit with some modifications. By 1918 there were 484 locomotives in the class. No.52400 was allocated to Sowerby Bridge MPD in June 1949, withdrawal from service being on 10th November 1960. *Colour Rail*

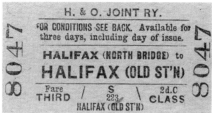

Fairburn 2-6-4T No.42073 is seen again, this time at Halifax with a Bradford Exchange to Rochdale parcels train. It often stopped at Mytholmroyd where the traffic comprised of day old chicks from Thornbers chicken hatchery. On the right of the picture is the chocolate factory of John Mackintosh Ltd. The author, who worked for some time at the adjacent Warner Swasey Machine Tool Ltd, would enjoy the variety of smells pervading the atmosphere depending on which flavour was being prepared. *Derek Phillips*

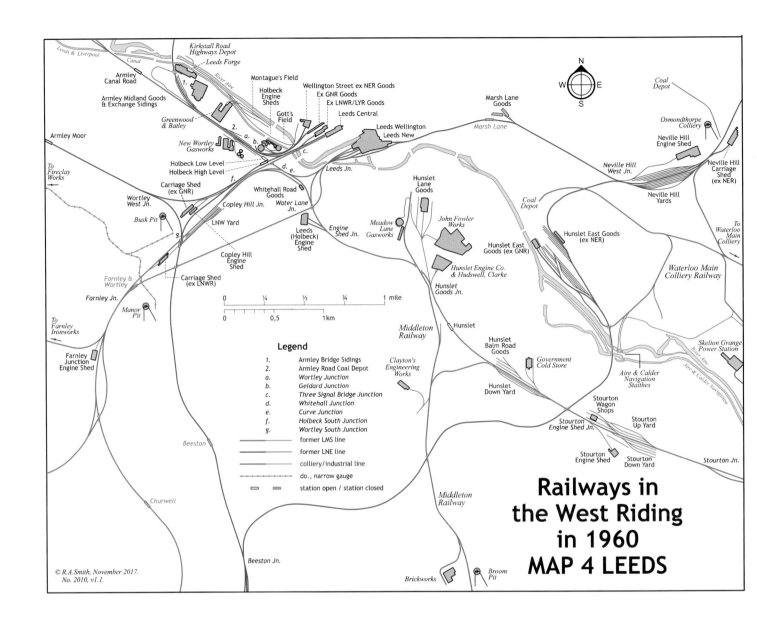

Kirkstall Road
Highways Depot
Leeds Forge
Leeds & Liverpool Canal
Armley Canal Road
Armley Midland Goods & Exchange Sidings
Montague's Field
Holbeck Engine Sheds
Wellington Street ex NER Goods
Ex GNR Goods
Ex LNWR/LYR Goods
Leeds Central
Gott's Field
Greenwood & Batley
Leeds Wellington
Leeds New
Armley Moor
New Wortley Gasworks
a.
b.
c.
Marsh Lane Goods
Marsh Lane
Coal Depot
Osmondthorpe Colliery
Neville Hill Engine Shed
Neville Hill West Jn.
Neville Hill Carriage Shed (ex NER)
To Fireclay Works
Holbeck Low Level
Holbeck High Level
d. e.
f.
Leeds Jn.
Neville Hill Yards
Carriage Shed (ex GNR)
Whitehall Road Goods
Water Lane Jn.
Hunslet Lane Goods
To Waterloo Main Colliery
Wortley West Jn.
Copley Hill Jn.
Coal Depot
Busk Pit
g.
LNW Yard
Engine Shed Jn.
Meadow Lane Gasworks
John Fowler Works
Hunslet East Goods (ex NER)
Copley Hill Engine Shed
Leeds (Holbeck) Engine Shed
Hunslet East Goods (ex GNR)
Waterloo Main Colliery Railway
Farnley & Wortley
Carriage Shed (ex LNWR)
Hunslet Engine Co. & Hudswell, Clarke
Skelton Grange Power Station
Farnley Jn.
Manor Pit
Hunslet Goods Jn.
Aire & Calder Navigation
To Farnley Ironworks
Middleton Railway
Hunslet
Aire & Calder Navigation Staithes
Farnley Junction Engine Shed
Clayton's Engineering Works
Hunslet Balm Road Goods
Government Cold Store
Stourton Wagon Shops
Beeston
Hunslet Down Yard
Stourton Up Yard
Churwell
Stourton Engine Shed Jn.
Stourton Down Yard
Stourton Jn.
Beeston Jn.
Middleton Railway
Stourton Engine Shed
Brickworks
Broom Pit

Legend

1. Armley Bridge Sidings
2. Armley Road Coal Depot
a. Wortley Junction
b. Geldard Junction
c. Three Signal Bridge Junction
d. Whitehall Junction
e. Curve Junction
f. Holbeck South Junction
g. Wortley South Junction

— former LMS line
— former LNE line
— colliery/industrial line
— do., narrow gauge
▭ ▬ station open / station closed

0 ¼ ½ ¾ 1 mile
0 0,5 1km

© R.A.Smith, November 2017.
No. 2010, v1.1.

Railways in the West Riding in 1960
MAP 4 LEEDS

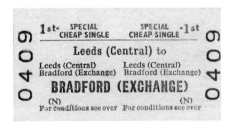

Fairburn 2-6-4T No.42138 is captured on the Midland side of Leeds City on 16th October 1963. The former Midland Railway Wellington station with its canopied platforms can be seen behind the loco. The Wellington station buildings at the far end of the platforms were modernised in the 1930s by the LMS which also built the Queens Hotel and Aire Street offices which dominate the skyline. These buildings now form part of the present Leeds station on which work had already started when this picture was taken. *David Mitchell*

<table>
<tr><td>0643</td><td>2nd - SINGLE</td><td>SINGLE - 2nd</td><td>0643</td></tr>
<tr><td></td><td colspan="2">Northallerton to</td><td></td></tr>
<tr><td></td><td>Northallerton
Leeds (City)</td><td>Northallerton
Leeds (City)</td><td></td></tr>
<tr><td></td><td colspan="2">LEEDS (CITY)
via Ripon or York</td><td></td></tr>
<tr><td></td><td>(N)   11/0</td><td>Fare   11/0   (N)</td><td></td></tr>
<tr><td></td><td colspan="2">For conditions see over   For conditions see over</td><td></td></tr>
</table>

Thompson Class B1 4-6-0 No.61129 makes a vigorous departure from Leeds Central on 30th September 1963 as it takes out the empty stock from a London train which had arrived behind Class A4 Pacific No.60006 *Sir Ralph Wedgwood*. Considering the size and importance of a city the size of Leeds it must have ranked as having two of the most unprepossessing stations anywhere on the British Railways' network. Having said that, because of the number of pre-grouping companies that served the Yorkshire metropolis, there was always a large variety of motive power still to be seen at both stations well into the BR era. Central was always the far more awkward of the two stations to operate, not least for the fact that even though it was once the departure point for the main London-bound expresses over the former GNR route, no train with more than seven or eight coaches could be accommodated in any of the platforms. *David Mitchell*

This view taken at Holbeck High Level on on 24th July 1966 sees Ivatt Class 4 2-6-0 No.43070 with the Bradford portion of a King's Cross express. Ivatt's Class 4 'Moguls' were a radical departure from traditional LMS designs actually being the last new design of locomotive for the LMS, although only three members of the 162-strong class were built before Nationalisation. Their high running plates became the pattern for the BR Standard classes that followed, moving away from more elegant designs to those of austerity. Only six members of this class survived into the last year of BR main line steam, the last to be withdrawn being No.43106 in June 1968 which survives in preservation on the Severn Valley Railway. No.43070 was reallocated to West Hartlepool in February 1967 and withdrawal came later that year in September. *Gerald Dixon*

Leeds Central was made no simpler to operate on its restricted site by also having to accommodate freight traffic. This view taken on 2nd October 1962 sees Copley Hill MPD's former LNER Class J50 0-6-0T No.68984 shunting vans. Together with classmate No.68988 they were also for many years employed on empty stock workings to Copley Hill. Originally designed for the GNR they were particularly associated with the West Riding and often referred to as 'Ardsley' tanks after the freight centre of that name between Leeds and Wakefield. Although they could be found operating in many former LNER areas it was Ardsley where many were first put to work. *Gavin Morrison*

This atmospheric night shot taken on 22nd April 1966 at Leeds Central sees the now-preserved Fairburn 2-6-4T No.42073 on station pilot duty. The last train left from Leeds Central on 29th April 1967. This was a Saturday and as there was no Sunday service, the station closed on 1 May 1967. The last train was an early evening service to Harrogate worked by the usual Birmingham RC&W DMU. Detonators were placed on the track by railway staff which exploded as the train rolled away from the platform and past the signal box with the final departure. *Gerald Dixon*

Another departure from Leeds, this time Jubilee Class 4-6-0 No.45562 *Alberta* prepares to depart from City with 1X10, a special train to Blackpool on 14th October 1966. Eight surviving members of the class soldiered on into 1967 working trains from the Leeds, Bradford and Wakefield areas, No.45562 being the last member of the class to be withdrawn. The remodelled Leeds City station was opened on 17th May 1967, when a commemorative plaque was unveiled by the Lord Mayor. Subsequently the station has again been rebuilt and significantly enlarged. *Peter Fitton*

This picture taken in June 1966 sees Ivatt Class 4 2-6-0 No.43137 crossing to the former GNR's passenger line at Wortley West Junction with the Bradford portion of a train from King's Cross which had been divided at Wakefield. The Great Northern Railway's empire in the West Riding had begun to crumble at the outbreak of the First World War. Severe pruning that had taken place in the 1950s and 1960s just left the route between Bradford, Leeds, Wakefield and Doncaster. Other towns in the West Riding remained rail served but by lines of the other pre-grouping companies with which the Great Northern had once competed. The GNR in the West Riding served mainly industrial regions with iron works, mills and numerous collieries. Its branch lines were a succession of sharp curves and steep gradients. No sooner had its passenger trains got going they had to stop for yet another station. In the 17 1/2 miles between Bradford Exchange and Wakefield there were fourteen intermediate halts. Similarly in the 9 1/2 miles between Bradford Exchange and Halifax North Bridge there were nine stops with a further eleven stops between Bradford Exchange and Keighley. For many years these local passenger workings were in the hands of former GNR Class N1 0-6-2Ts. *David Mitchell*

The name Copley Hill was more readily associated with the Great Northern system but 'The Wessie' also had extensive yards and a carriage depot there. The former LNWR route to Leeds which was known to generations of railwaymen as 'The Wessie' carried the principal Trans-Pennine expresses much as it does today. Here Ivatt Class 4 2-6-0 No.43036 is seen marshalling a train in the yards at Copley Hill on 17th May 1963. *David Mitchell*

This view, showing the west end of Copley Hill motive power depot on 12th June 1963, sees Class J50/1 0-6-0T No.68892 in the shed yard. The five road shed was situated in the triangle formed by the Doncaster and Bradford lines, and the Wortley curve which linked the two and provided a direct route from Doncaster to Bradford. The depot, which had been modernised in the early 1950s, was coded 37B in the Ardsley district of the Eastern Region until 1956 when it became 56C in the North Eastern Region's newly formed Wakefield district. Beyond the railings at the right of the shed is the main line from Leeds Central to Doncaster and King's Cross. *David Mitchell*

An unidentified Class Q6 0-8-0 is captured climbing through the cavernous depths of Marsh Lane Cutting with an eastbound freight on 28th April 1966. The construction of the Marsh Lane Cutting and tunnel through Richmond Hill had led to the loss of many lives and it quickly gained a bad reputation due to locomotive smoke and darkness. Whitewash and copper reflectors were added to improve lighting although the line was eventually widened and the tunnel opened out in 1894. This was primarily to allow increased traffic movements after Neville Hill engine sheds were expanded. The opening out of the tunnel resulted in the most impressive civil engineering along the line, with a deep cutting and a series of impressive cross bridges. A station was originally located on the west side of the tunnel at Marsh Lane, this closing in 1958. Neville Hill depot is located just north of the line, east of the cutting. *Gerald Dixon*

Another Class Q6 0-8-0 is seen, this time at Cross Gates, as it heads a Leeds bound train on 25th September 1963. At its peak, Cross Gates had four through lines, a junction to Wetherby, and various goods sidings; the route to Wetherby being the first railway in the area to be closed under Beeching's infamous axe. Its cutting can still be seen from the station platforms. Dedicated sidings also existed to serve local collieries and the Royal Ordnance Factory at Barnbow and this location was initially considered for the joint LNER-LMS locomotive testing station before the site at Rugby was chosen. *David Mitchell*

Above: Stanier Class 5 No.44824 is seen passing Gelderd Junction in Leeds with a train from the Harrogate line on 18th February 1967. Behind the locomotive can be seen the Grade II listed roundhouse built for the Leeds and Thirsk Railway which later amalgamated with the Leeds and Selby and the York and North Midland to become the North Eastern Railway. The roundhouse was designed with a single entrance track with 20 stabling bays radiating around a central turntable measuring approximately 42ft 6in. By 1889 the roundhouse was far too small for larger modern engines and was closed. It was then used as a drill hall for the Leeds Rifles until 1916 before becoming the home of Marshalls Engineers. Leeds Commercial Ltd van and truck hire, who have occupied the property since 1969, invite the public to view the roundhouse during National Heritage Weekend each year and the historical information provided here is taken from a leaflet supplied at one of these events. *David Mitchell*

Opposite: High above the gas lit back streets of Leeds, Jubilee Class 4-6-0 No.45562 *Alberta* is seen at Holbeck on Saturday 30th July 1966 as it works the SO 9.8am Leeds to Poole train which it will take as far as Nottingham via Huddersfield, Penistone and Sheffield. In addition to being the last working member of this once prestigious class of locomotives, No.45562 also became the last steam engine to haul the Royal Train in BR days, conveying the Duke of Edinburgh from York to Nidd Bridge. The Royal Train had arrived in York from Windsor on 30th May 1967 behind two Type 2 diesels. The Jubilee then took the train on to Nidd Bridge via Knaresborough and Starbeck after which No.45562 worked the empty train to Ripon in order to run round. The loco worked the train tender first to Starbeck and on to York whence the train was diesel hauled to Sheffield to collect the Duke of Edinburgh in the evening. After withdrawal from service in November 1967 *Alberta* was stored until January 1968 at Leeds Holbeck MPD before being moved to Normanton until April 1968. The loco was broken up at Cashmore's in Great Bridge in May 1968. *Gerald Dixon*

Above: Sitting around the turntable inside the roundhouse at Leeds Holbeck MPD on 1st August 1965 are ex-LMS Stanier Class 5 4-6-0 No.45394, Ivatt Class 4 2-6-0 No.43124 and ex-LMS Stanier Class 4 2-6-4T No.42622. Holbeck was the Midland Railway's main shed serving Leeds. Situated on the main line from Whitehall Junction towards Stourton it was home to many top-link passenger locomotives. In 1959 it was home to almost twenty Jubilee and five Royal Scot Class 4-6-0s. In later years it was well known amongst railway enthusiasts as the home of the last members of the Jubilee Class 4-6-0s such as *Alberta* and *Kolhapur* which had survived the remainder of the class by several months running through the summer of 1967. They were kept in immaculate condition by the nefarious nocturnal activities of the MNA enthusiast group; their exploits being well recorded. Their workings perhaps marked the final swansong of steam operations in the West Riding. *Bill Wright*

Opposite: This stunning photograph not only captures the atmosphere inside Leeds Holbeck MPD on 28th July 1963 but also the detailed MIdland Railway architecture forming the entrance to the roundhouse. Locos visible in this view are BR Standard Class 4 2-6-4T No.80116, ex-LMS Stanier Class 5 4-6-0 No.44862 and Ivatt Class 4 2-6-0 No.43039. The last steam shed in Leeds, Holbeck closed on 30th September 1967, after which all such locomotives visiting the city had to be serviced at Normanton, 14 miles away. The last steam engine to leave Holbeck under its own power was Stanier Class 5 4-6-0 No.45428, bound for preservation in Birmingham on 24th August 1968. *Gerald Dixon*

Leeds Holbeck MPD's No 1 type concrete coaling tower looms in the darkness in this picture taken on 10th December 1965. The coaling tower, which was demolished on 10th October 1966, had two bunkers that could hold 300 tons of coal and was able to service two engines at a time. Highlighted in the foreground is Stanier Class 5 4-6-0 No.45063 with a pair of BR Sulzer Type 2s parked in the mist behind. No.45063 spent many years allocated to Farnley Junction MPD and after a brief spell at Leeds Neville Hill shed was allocated to Leeds Holbeck depot in June 1964 where it remained until withdrawn from service in November 1966. *Gerald Dixon*

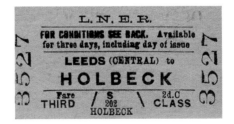

The largest steam shed in the Leeds area was the former North Eastern Railway running shed at Neville Hill. Opened in 1904 the layout of the original shed followed North Eastern practice; a large building containing four roundhouses with radiating stalls, each interlinked beneath one roof. At any given period during the immediate post-war years, the shed's usual allocation of engines consisted of five A3s, ten B16s, thirteen B1s, two D20s, four D49s, eleven J39s, five N13s, two A8s and four G5s. The shed was reduced to half its size during the late 1950s and demolished in its entirety in September 1970. Upon nationalisation in 1948, BR's power classification code was adopted from the old LMS system using the numbers 0-9 to indicate power, based on tractive effort calculations; plus the letters 'P' for passenger, 'F' for freight and later the designation 'MT' for mixed traffic was added. This identification system was used on the LMR and Southern Region only. Meanwhile the Western Region continued to use the old GWR classification code, with the power rating based on letters A-E and coloured dots for route availability, while on the Eastern and North Eastern Region locomotives, the route availability code (RA1 to 9) was preferred. In this view of the cramped interior taken on 28th July 1963 can be seen Class A1 Pacific No.60146 *Peregrine* together with an unidentified Gresley Class V2 and Raven Class Q6 0-8-0. By 1987, the depot had an allocation of Class 08 shunters with Class 101, 108, 110, 111, 141, 142, 144 and 150 DMUs and Class 254 HSTs also being allocated. *Gerald Dixon*

This June 1957 image sees an unidentified Hunt Class D49 4-4-0 with a short train for Harrogate crossing Arthington Viaduct. Also known as Castley Viaduct and listed as the Wharfedale Viaduct it carries the Harrogate line across the Wharfe valley between Arthington and Castley. It is a Grade II listed structure. The viaduct was built, between 1845 and 1849, in a curve some 500 yards in length, with 21 semi-circular arches on high piers. Construction was supervised by Chief Engineer of the Leeds & Thirsk Railway, Thomas Grainger, who built the line from Leeds to Stockton-on-Tees via Harrogate and Thirsk. The foundation stone was laid on 31st March 1846 by Henry Cooper Marshall, Chairman of Leeds & Thirsk Railway and the line opened on 10th July 1849 when the nearby Bramhope Tunnel, another key component of the line, was complete. In excess of 50,000 tons of stone were used in the viaduct's construction. *David Kelso*

Class 4F 0-6-0 No.44186 is approaching Harrogate from the north with a van train in this view taken c.1958. Harrogate's first railway station, Brunswick, was the terminus of York and North Midland Railway's branch line and the first train arrived there on 20th July 1848. The station was situated on the site where Trinity Church now stands, close to the Prince of Wales roundabout and some distance from either High or Low Harrogate. When the new line of the North Eastern Railway entered Harrogate via a cutting through The Stray, Brunswick closed and the first train into the town centre station was on 1st August 1862. *Derek Penney*

This picture taken c1960 sees a Class B1 4-6-0 marshalling a short freight at Pateley Bridge. The line from Harrogate lost its passenger service after Class G5 0-4-4T No.67253 left Harrogate for the last time at 5.35pm on Saturday 31st March 1951. For almost 30 years prior to closure No.67253 had been the regular engine on the branch and had been accommodated in a shed at Pateley Bridge which housed just one locomotive and employed two drivers, two fireman and a cleaner who worked alone at night. During routine maintenance at Starbeck or longer stays in works, a substitute engine was sent to Pateley Bridge, usually another Class G5. *David Mitchell*

Another view at Pateley Bridge taken some years later, on 11th March 1964, sees Class K1 2-6-0 No.62046 taking water with the ruins of the signal box being visible behind the locomotive's tender. Whilst the line lost its passenger services in 1951 the closure of the line and the station to all traffic was not until October 1964. *David Mitchell*

This view from the north end of Wetherby station taken on 25th September 1963 sees the preserved Class K4 2-6-0 No.3442 *The Great Marquess* propelling an inspection saloon which is signalled for the Church Fenton line with the line to Harrogate diverging to the left. Out of sight on the right of the picture was the livestock bay with the three-arm signal controlling the exit from the up platform in the down direction. Also evident is the Spofforth Hill road bridge spanning the tracks at the junction. In March 1963, the Beeching report called for the withdrawal of passenger services on the Leeds-Wetherby-Harrogate and Church Fenton-Wetherby lines and the closure of their stations. A headline, 'First Lamb to the Beeching Slaughter', mentioned that 'No Regular Passengers Object' at the Inquiry, which was the case for only the Church Fenton line. A decision was reached on 24th October 1963 after a three-month enquiry. The axe fell on 6th January 1964 for passenger services on both lines, although goods traffic continued on the Leeds line for a further four months until 27th April 1964. Goods services on the Church Fenton line continuing until 4th April 1966. *David Mitchell*

Passing the Goods Yard at Tadcaster on 21st July 1964 is Ivatt Class 4 2-6-0 No.43097. The station at Tadcaster had closed to passenger traffic earlier that year on 6th January; goods traffic ending on 30th November 1966. The station at Tadcaster opened in 1848 as part of the Harrogate to Church Fenton line of the York and North Midland Railway. Another line from Copmanthorpe to Cross Gates was authorised in 1846 and would have joined the line from Harrogate just north of Tadcaster station, but aside from a bridge across the River Wharfe which still stands today it was never built.
David Mitchell

Another Ivatt Class 4 2-6-0 is featured here, this time No.43084 is captured at Church Fenton as it heads a lightweight parcels working from York to Normanton on 5th July 1967. The station at Church Fenton was opened by the York and North Midland Railway in 1839 but lost its East Coast Main Line status in 1871 when the new direct line from York to Doncaster was opened, trains from London to Harrogate continuing to call. Yet another addition to the list of routes serving the station came in 1879 when the Swinton and Knottingley Joint Railway line via Pontefract Baghill and Ferrybridge was opened. In connection with the quadrupling of the lines the present station was opened in 1904 slightly south of the second station. *Peter Fitton*

This stunning action shot of Class A4 Pacific No.60009 *Union of South Africa* was taken at Selby on 24th October 1964 as it heads the northbound 'The Jubilee Requiem, 1964' railtour which ran between London and Newcastle. Organised jointly by the Railway Correspondence & Travel Society and the Stephenson Locomotive Society it was probably the last of Gresley's famous A4s to be seen at King's Cross. The special was twenty minutes late through Grantham owing to a broken rail at High Dyke. Built by the London and North Eastern Railway (LNER) in 1937 at Doncaster and originally numbered 4488, it was named after the then newly formed *Union of South Africa*. It was allocated to Haymarket shed in Edinburgh from new and on 20th May 1962 it had its only shed transfer to Aberdeen Ferryhill. It was also the last loco to be overhauled at Doncaster whilst in service and was withdrawn from British Railways on 1 June 1966. *Derek Penney*

The locomotive depot at Goole is clearly illustrated in this view taken on 9th April 1967 where a number of WD 2-8-0s can be seen. Often perceived as a land-locked county, the West Riding of Yorkshire stretched as far east as Goole which falls into the area covered by this book. The docks at Goole were rapidly developed in the mid-19th century by the patronage of the Lancashire & Yorkshire Railway primarily for the shipment of coal. *W.Potter/KRM*

The centenary of Doncaster Works in September 1953 provided a tailor-made opportunity For Mr. Alan Pegler and his associates to achieve their ambition to steam former Great Northern Atlantics again. The special train hauled by the small-boilered 'Klondyke' No.990 *Henry Oakley* and the large-boilered No.251 from King's Cross to Doncaster was packed with over 400 enthusiasts and is seen here on the approaches to Doncaster. *Jim Jarvis/KRM*

In its last summer of operation and with only a passing glance from trainspotters Class A3 Pacific No.60081 *Shotover* is captured at York with an up express in July 1962. The Gresley Pacific, originally Class A1 No.2580, was built by the North British Locomotive Co, Works No 23118, in November 1924. It was rebuilt and re-classified to Class A3 in February 1928, renumbered 81 in 1946, later becoming BR No.60081 on 3rd June 1948. It was allocated new to Heaton, then went on loan to Haymarket, and its later sheds were Gateshead, Heaton again, Neville Hill, York, Gateshead again and finally back to Neville Hill where it spent its final thirteen years up to withdrawal on 1st October 1962. It was cut up at Doncaster Works. The loco achieved fame on 1st May 1928 when it hauled the inaugural southbound non-stop running of the Flying Scotsman, departing from Edinburgh Waverley at 10am, with No.4472 *Flying Scotsman* hauling the corresponding northbound train from King's Cross on the same day. *David Kelso*

Gresley Class A8 4-6-2T No.69860 stands at the north end of York station with a Scarborough coast lines express working on a summer Saturday in August 1958. Originally constructed as 4-4-4 tanks the Class A8s were built for short-distance passenger work. In 1931 it was decided that the locos might advantageously be rebuilt with an extra pair of driving wheels. All 45 members of the class were so rebuilt and proved very succesful on the many difficult branches in the north east. *David Kelso*

2nd-SINGLE   SINGLE-2nd
Pontefract (Baghill) to   Pontefract (Baghill)
York   York
YORK
via Church Fenton
(N)   3/9   Fare   3/9   (N)
For conditions see over   For conditions see over

One of two Class J72s repainted in NER green livery for use as station pilots at York and Newcastle in 1960, No.68736 is seen at York in July 1960. In 1961 it moved to Newcastle, remaining there until withdrawn in September 1963. *KRM*

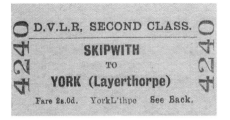

LNER Class J21 0-6-0 No.65064 stands at York Layerthorpe, the terminus of the Derwent Valley Light Railway, on 17th May 1958 with a Branch Line Society excursion having arrived after running non-stop the nearly 16 miles from the southern terminus of the railway at Cliff Common. The loco was withdrawn in September 1958. *David Kelso*

One of a number of locos prepared for the exhibition at Doncaster Works in September 1953 celebrating its centenary was Class A1 Pacific No.60118 *Archibald Sturrock*. Sturrock was Locomotive Superintendent of the Great Northern Railway from 1850 until c.1866, having from 1840 been Daniel Gooch's assistant on the Great Western Railway. *Jim Jarvis/KRM*

Seen in Crimpsall erecting shop at Doncaster Works, Class A4 Pacific No.60004 *William Whitelaw* is receiving its last General Repair in November 1962. Entering service in December 1937 as LNER No.4462 it carried the name *Great Snipe* until June 1941 when during a General Repair it was selected to be re-named *William Whitelaw*. *Derek Penney*

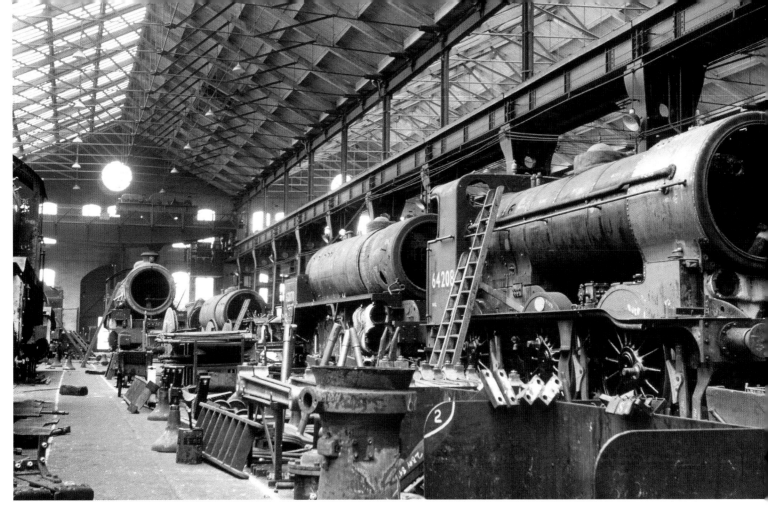

Crimpsall erecting shop was added to Doncaster Works in 1901. This interior view taken on 20th April 1958 shows locomotives undergoing heavy repairs; Gresley Class J6 0-6-0 No.64208 is visiting from Ardsley MPD and the Peppercorn Class K1 Mogul behind, No.62070 sent from March depot, will be re-allocated to Stratford when it leaves 'The Plant'. *W.Potter/KRM*

Also on exhibition at Doncaster Works in September 1953 was Class V2 2-6-2 No.60862. Built at Darlington Works in June 1939 it was fitted with a double-chimney during 1960/61 before being withdrawn from service in June 1963. *Jim Jarvis/KRM*

This undated image taken at Wakefield Kirkgate sees bunker-first Stanier 2-6-4T No.42650 which has arrived with the Bradford portion of an express for King's Cross. *Derek Phillips*

A view taken in the up yard at Wakefield MPD on 30th October 1966 sees the following line up of locomotives :-

From left to right are :-
Ex-LMS Class 5 4-6-0 No.45211
Ex-LMS Class 5 4-6-0 No.44944
Ex-LMS Ivatt 4MT Mogul No.43070
Ex-LMS Jubilee 4-6-0 No.45739 *Ulster*
Ex-LNER B1 4-6-0 No.61173
WD 8F 2-8-0 No.90236
Ex-LMS Stanier 8F 2-8-0 No.48267
Bill Wright

The two guards smiling for the camera add a human element to this picture of bunker-first WD 8F 2-8-0 No.90363 as it departs from Wakefield Kirkgate, engine and brake van, on 2nd January 1967. The first direct rail link to the city came with the opening of the Leeds & Manchester Railway's line from Hebden Bridge to Goose Hill Junction on 8th October 1840; the opening of the line giving Wakefield its first station, later known as Kirkgate. The construction of the Wakefield, Pontefract & Goole Railway gave a direct link with Goole but by the time the line opened in 1848 both the WPG and the M&L had been absorbed into the Lancashire & Yorkshire Railway. The second major pre-Grouping company to arrive in Wakefield was the Great Northern which reached its temporary station (later Westgate) through the offices of the Bradford, Wakefield & Leeds Railway in 1857. *Bill Wright*

The cooling towers of Wakefield power station dominate the background of this picture showing the shed yard at Wakefield MPD on 28th July 1963. Originally built closer to the station at Kirkgate the depot was rebuilt and expanded around the time of the First World War to cope with the increase in coal traffic from the area's many pits. It was always a predominantly freight depot although in later years it did have a few passenger engines, the bulk of its allocation being made up of WD Austerity 2-8-os. Plans to convert it to a diesel maintenance depot rather than Healey Mills did not materialise with the shed remaining all steam until its closure on 3rd June 1967. After closure the depot presented a grim sight with lines of withdrawn engines on their way to scrapyards in the North East. Becoming a wagon repair depot until final closure in 1984 the structure survived until it was demolished in 1993. *Gerald Dixon*

With Wakefield MPD's coaling tower No.3 on the left an unidentified WD 2-8-o passes with a loaded coal train whilst another member of the class passes light engine in the opposite direction. A 24th June 1966 picture. *Gerald Dixon*

Goole MPD's WD 2-8-0 No.90406 is only a few minutes away from the depot at Wakefield as it passes Walton, between Oakenshaw and Crofton junctions, with a loaded coal train on 8th February 1967. During the 1950s and 1960s the WD 2-8-0s were a common sight in both Lancashire and Yorkshire. In 1950, 136 members of this class were allocated to 10 former Lancashire & Yorkshire Railway sheds but by 1959, 193 were allocated to 14 'Lanky' depots. Even as late as 1965, these sheds had 106 available for traffic. The groundwork for this section of line had been prepared by the Wakefield, Pontefract and Goole Railway but this had been absorbed by the L&YR before it opened to traffic in 1848. Out of sight under the left hand arch of the bridge, out of picture, passed the L&YR connection to the one-time Midland Railway main line from Sheffield to Leeds.
Peter Fitton

Carrying the earlier BR lion and wheel emblem, Stanier 8F 2-8-0 48130 of Royston shed passes Royston Junction signal box on the up slow line with a Class A goods, possibly from Normanton to Carlton North sidings. The tracks on the left form the Midland Railway's ill fated attempt to reach Bradford, a scheme which got no further than Dewsbury and ended up with a connection onto the L&Y at Thornhill. In addition to brief allocations to both Wakefield and Leeds Holbeck depots the remainder of this loco's career was divided between Royston and Stourton depots before withdrawal in February 1967. Breaking up was undertaken at Drapers yard in Hull. An August 1958 picture. *David Kelso*

Tender first Johnson Midland Railway Class 3F 0-6-0 No.43250 of Royston shed passes Royston Junction on the up fast with a train of empty coal wagons. The locomotive is crossing the Barnsley branch of the disused Aire & Calder navigation and is about to pass under the bridge carrying the Great Central Railway branch from Wharncliffe Woodmoor to reach the WR & G Joint Railway at Nostell. This branch which ran via Staincross was later closed on 31st July 1961. In the background is the Monkton Main Colliery and Coke Works. An August 1958 picture. *David Kelso*

Another August 1958 picture sees LMS 4F 0-6-0 No.44223 of Sheffield Millhouses as it heads an Express Freight past Royston Junction signal box with the Dewsbury branch to Thornhill curving away to the left. *David Kelso*

This November 1963 view taken at Royston MPD depicts the usual Sunday line up of the depot's allocation of Stanier 8F 2-8-os. Their main weekday duties were the haulage of coal traffic over mineral or branch lines nearest to the sorting sidings. *P.J. Hughes/Colour Rail*

Class J39 0-6-0 No.64902 is nearest to the camera in this view taken at Barnsley MPD in August 1959. Exchange station is on the left with its single platform only on the down side. It was used jointly by the L&Y and the MS&L (GC) until the Midland built their own superior structure on an embankment nearby calling it Court House which opened in 1870. The MS&L willingly paid for half of the construction costs in order to be able to use it and get out of Exchange which was doing very little for their image. Before we leave Exchange mention should be made of the passenger service to Wakefield via Nostell, a GC venture which vanished in the early 1930s. *Colour Rail*

Doncaster MPD's Class B1 4-6-0 No.61121 approaches Mexborough station with a freight from the Wath line on 11th September 1963. It is passing Mexborough No.2 signal box on the right with the lines to Swinton diverging to the left. The box was abolished on Sunday 26th July 1970 when existing semaphore signals were removed and new colour light signals were brought into use with full track circuiting. From this date Mexborough No.3 signal box was then renamed Mexborough signal box.
Neville Simms

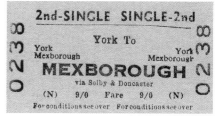

is view of the shed yard taken at Mexborough on 10th May 1959 can be seen a number of Ex-WD Austerity 2-8-0s, several Class O4 2-8-0s and a ary Class J11/3 'Pom-Pom' No.64393. The Great Central Railway (GCR) Class 9J (LNER J11) was Robinson's first goods locomotive design. An initial batch rty J11s were built by Neilson, Reid & Co in 1901-2. These were quickly followed by eleven further batches built between 1902 and 1910. Most of these much smaller, although a large batch of forty eight was built at Gorton in 1906-8. Beyer, Peacock & Co, Vulcan Foundry and the Yorkshire Engine Co. built some of the batches. A total of 174 J11s were built. The J11s quickly acquired the nickname of 'Pom-Poms' due to the similarity of their exhaust to that of the 'Pom-Pom' quick-firing gun used in the South African War. Thompson chose a modified J11 to be one of his LNER post-war standard es. The main modification was the fitting of long-travel piston valves similar to those used on the J39s, but with a smaller diameter. The new valves red the boiler to be pitched higher, and in-turn a shorter chimney to be fitted. Between 1942 and 1953, a total of thirty one J11s were rebuilt with piston valves. The original standardisation plan also called for round-topped fireboxes, but this part of the plan was not implemented. Most of the notives stabled at Mexborough were used for hauling coal trains. The coal originated from the many collieries in the South Yorkshire coalfield and ns of coal were despatched to locations all over the country. However, the main destinations were the industries and power stations in Lancashire. the opening of the Wath marshalling yard in 1907, Mexborough supplied locomotives for collecting wagons from the collieries, for re-marshalling e wagons at Wath and for hauling coal trains over the steeply-graded Woodhead route across the Pennines into Lancashire. In the 1920s, the depot the stabling point for what was then the most powerful locomotive in the UK, the London & North Eastern Railway's Class U1 Garratt. It was used for ing heavy coal trains up the Worsborough incline on the Woodhead route *W.Potter/KRM*

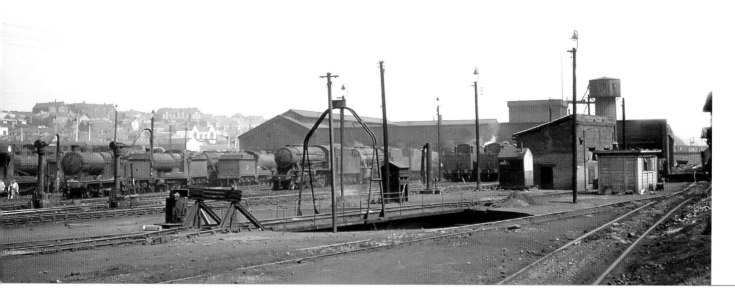

The SO 9.08am Poole to Leeds train is seen being hauled through Silkstone by Jubilee Class 4-6-0 No.45647 *Sturdee* in the summer of 1966. The first station on this site, simply known as Silkstone, was opened on 1st November 1855 and rebuilt on the same site in the last quarter of the 19th century in the 'Double Pavilion' style favoured by the Manchester, Sheffield and Lincolnshire Railway. The present station, opened in May 1983, is now known as Silkstone Common. *David Mitchell*

This train is seen again passing the signal box at Dodworth. The crossing and the access to the local colliery was originally adjacent to the level crossing which took the main Manchester road (the present-day A628 road) through the village. It was controlled from an earlier box, of Manchester, Sheffield and Lincolnshire Railway (MS&LR) hipped-roof design, set by the crossing but was demolished by a derailment on 24th January 1955. The rebuilt box seen here was a brick built, flat roofed affair. This still stands, but is now disused, the crossing being remotely operated from Barnsley Power Signal Box (P.S.B.). *David Mitchell*

In July 1957 Ex-LNER Class J39 0-6-0 No.64794 joins the West Riding & Grimsby Joint main line between Wakefield Westgate and Doncaster at Hare Park Junction with an Express Goods from the former Lancashire & Yorkshire Railway's Wakefield Kirkgate to Pontefract line, where it joins the WR&GJ at Crofton Junction. The first locomotive of the class was completed at Darlington in September 1926, almost exactly one year after an original outline drawing was prepared by the drawing office. The first 44 were completed during 1926/27 and were an immediate sucess, a further 79 being built by 1929. Despite a reduction of freight traffic in the early 1930s caused by a severe industrial recession, 101 more were built by 1936 with another 47 being constructed in 1937/8, with a final batch of 18 in 1941 bringing the total to 289, the largest Gresley locomotive class. All were erected at Darlington apart from 28 being purchased from Beyer Peacock in 1936/37 which in part was to provide work for private locomotive manufacturers affected by the trade recession. In addition to being operated on all routes for freight work they were also used to a considerable extent in passenger service, especially at weekends when freight movement was greatly reduced. Allocated throughout the Eastern, North Eastern and Scottish regions of BR the class remained intact until May 1959. *David Kelso*

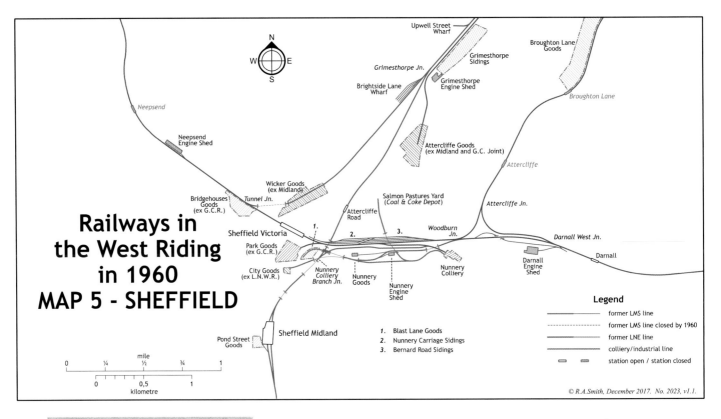

Railways in the West Riding in 1960
MAP 5 - SHEFFIELD

Upwell Street Wharf

Broughton Lane Goods

Grimesthorpe Sidings

Grimesthorpe Jn.

Grimesthorpe Engine Shed

Brightside Lane Wharf

Broughton Lane

Neepsend

Neepsend Engine Shed

Attercliffe Goods (ex Midland and G.C. Joint)

Attercliffe

Wicker Goods (ex Midland)

Salmon Pastures Yard (Coal & Coke Depot)

Attercliffe Jn.

Bridgehouses Goods (ex G.C.R.)

Tunnel Jn.

Attercliffe Road

Sheffield Victoria

1.

2.

3.

Woodburn Jn.

Darnall West Jn.

Park Goods (ex G.C.R.)

Darnall

Darnall Engine Shed

City Goods (ex L.N.W.R.)

Nunnery Colliery Branch Jn.

Nunnery Goods

Nunnery Engine Shed

Nunnery Colliery

Pond Street Goods

Sheffield Midland

1. Blast Lane Goods
2. Nunnery Carriage Sidings
3. Bernard Road Sidings

Legend

———	former LMS line
- - - -	former LMS line closed by 1960
———	former LNE line
	colliery/industrial line
▭ ▭	station open / station closed

© R.A.Smith, December 2017. No. 2023, v1.1.

mile
0 ¼ ½ ¾ 1

0 0,5 1
kilometre

2nd- SPECIAL CHEAP SINGLE   SPECIAL CHEAP SINGLE -2nd

5987   5987

Elsecar & Hoyland to

Elsecar & Hoyland Sheffield (Midland)   Elsecar & Hoyland Sheffield (Midland)

SHEFFIELD (MIDLAND)

(E)   (E)

For conditions see over   For conditions see over

Gone are the rows of begrimed terrace houses above Sheffield Midland station in this picture dated 25th April 1965. They were replaced by the Park Hill flats which dwarfed the station and became an iconic symbol of 1960s Sheffield. The station was given two extra platforms and a new frontage in 1905 at a cost of £215,000. The enlargements consisted of creating an island platform out of the old platform 1 and building a new platform 1 and a new entrance. The works were overseen by the Chief Architect to the Midland Railway, Charles Trubshaw. These changes were criticised at the time for their lack of stature and such grand features as a clocktower. *Tommy Tomalin*

Still carrying the old BR Lion & Wheel emblem Sheffield Millhouses MPD's Jubilee 4-6-0 No.45594 *Bhopal* climbs the 1 in 100 away from Sheffield Midland with a Bristol express in the summer of 1959. With the introduction of diesel traction to Midland Line services No.45594 became one of the first casualties, being reallocated to Carnforth MPD at the end of 1959 where it remained until it returned to the Sheffield area being allocated to Canklow MPD in December 1961. Other moves on the Midland lines came in 1961 with the displacement of most of the Royal Scots from passenger work at Kentish Town, Nottingham and Trafford Park. This move was followed later that year when Jubilees were eliminated from other principal Midland main line depots. Final withdrawal was from Sheffield Darnall in December 1962. *Derek Penney*

This superb portrait taken outside Sheffield Millhouses shed shows Bristol Barrow Road MPD's Patriot Class 4-6-0 *Lady Godiva* before working south with a Sheffield Midland to Gloucester train in the summer of 1959. The class was withdrawn over a two year period between 1960 and 1962, each loco having covered around 1.3 million miles. The last two to be withdrawn, No.45543 *Home Guard* and No.45550, were in good condition on withdrawal but unfortunately it was too early for them to be considered for preservation. Today this omission from the 1960s has been rectified with the 'new-build project' of No.5551 which was originally based on the Llangollen Railway in Denbighshire, Wales. Unlike other new builds this engine will be a replica of the original engine which was withdrawn in June 1962 and scrapped in October of the same year. Unlike the original engine, which never received a name during its career with the LMS and BR, the replica will be named *The Unknown Warrior*. The original No.5551/45551 was built at Crewe Works in May 1934, most members of the class were given names, but No.45551 and nine other class members weren't named. Sheds that it was allocated to over the years included: Crewe North, Carlisle Upperby, Camden, Willesden and Edge Hill. Edge Hill was the last shed it was allocated to, being transferred there in June 1961 and remaining there for twelve months until withdrawal. It was also one of thirty four members of it's class to be kept in it's original unrebuilt condition prior to it's final withdrawal in June 1962, it's final working life was twenty eight years and one month. It was later cut up for scrap in October of the same year at her birthplace Crewe Works. No.45519, however, survived in operation at Bristol Barrow Road where it was allocated in November 1958, final withdrawal being in March 1962. *Derek Penney*

Nottingham MPD's former Midland Railway Class 2P 4-4-0 No.40542 is portrayed outside Sheffield Millhouses shed on 10th May 1959. The Midland Railway 483 Class 4-4-0 was designed by Samuel W. Johnson for passenger work on the Midland Railway, the design forming the basis of the later LMS Class 2P 4-4-0. The London, Midland and Scottish Railway (LMS) inherited three batches of these locomotives, most of them passing into British Railways (BR) ownership in 1948. *W. Potter/KRM*

A general view of Sheffield Millhouses MPD also taken on 10th May 1959 with ex-LMS Class 2P No.40542 (seen above), ex-LMS Class 2 2-6-2T No.41245 alongside BR Standard Class 5 No.73065. Built by the Midland Railway in 1901 as Ecclesall engine shed to serve the Midland Main Line it was renamed Millhouses in 1920. It mainly provided passenger locomotives for top link expresses being home to some of the Midland Line's finest engines as well as a number of antique passenger tanks. Built next to Millhouses railway station it had eight dead end roads and could handle about forty steam locomotives. The depot came under the control of the Eastern Region being coded 41C, being subordinate to the former LNER depot at Darnall. Soon after this event the Sheffield district depots were rationalised particularly with the dieselisation of former MIdland Railway lines, Millhouses shed closing on the 1st January 1962. For many years afterwards the shed survived in private industrial use and still stood in 2012. Today a Tesco car park occupies the yard. *W.Potter/KRM*

Coming into Sheffield Victoria station past No.4 box, Class D11/1 No.62667 *Somme* is arriving with a Class B passenger service, probably from Retford, sometime in 1958. Whilst the new Class B1 4-6-0s quickly replaced the older Great Central passenger locos in the 1940s, the 'Large Director' D11s survived. In BR days most of the D11/2s were in Scotland but the eleven D11/1s were mainly allocated to Lincoln, Northwich, Immingham or Trafford Park. When displaced by diesels, they were transferred to Sheffield Darnall and retained for additional summer services until 1960. *Derek Penney*

Also in 1958, sister loco No.62665 *Mons* is captured with a local for Retford, halfway between Sheffield Victoria and Woodburn Junction. One of the first eleven 'Large Directors' built at Gorton between 1919 and 1922, the Class D11 locomotives had several design modifications to the Class D10s, the easiest way to distinguish them was that the later type had cab windows. A further 24 engines were added to the fleet by the LNER in 1924 for service in Scotland, the complete class of 35 passing into BR ownership in 1948. The last member of this class survived until late 1961/early 1962, the first of the Gorton-built locos No.506 *Butler Henderson* being preserved. *Derek Penney*

This superb portrait depicts Class B17/6 No.61641 *Gayton Hall* making use of the turntable at Sheffield Victoria in September 1958. The first ten locomotives of this class were built by the North British Locomotive Co (Works Nos. 23803-12) during November and December 1928 and were allocated the running numbers 2800-9. Five further orders were placed with Darlington Works between December 1928 and March 1935 for a further fifty-two locomotives to be delivered between August 1930 and June 1936. A final batch of eleven was ordered from Robert Stephenson and Co in February 1936 (Works Nos. 4124-34) for delivery between January and July 1937; resulting in a total of 73 B17s built. The first ten by the North British Locomotive Co were designated B17, later B17/1. The second and third batches had boilers supplied by Armstrong Whitworth and different springing and became B17/2. The next two batches had the different springing and were designated B17/3. However, as the locomotives passed through works the original springs were replaced by those of the later design and in 1937 the three sub-classes were merged into B17/1. The final Darlington batch introduced in 1936, and those built by Robert Stephenson and Co had 4,200-imperial-gallon (19,000 l; 5,000 US gal), 7.5-long-ton (7.6 t) tenders and were intended for use in the North Eastern area of the LNER: these were designated B17/4. In September 1937, two locomotives (Nos. 2859 *Norwich City* and 2870 *Tottenham Hotspur*, were streamlined in the manner of the LNER Class A4s, renamed *East Anglian* and *City of London* and intended for use on the 'East Anglian' train. They were designated B17/5. However, the streamlining was cladding for publicity purposes only and had little effect on the overall speed of the locomotive. By 1951 both engines had been stripped of the streamlining altogether. Between 1943 and 1957 most of the surviving members of the class were rebuilt with a LNER 100A boiler with increased pressure and were designated B17/6. *Derek Penney*

In the summer of 1958 March MPD's Class B17/6 No.61657 *Doncaster Rovers* is captured at Rotherwood outside Sheffield having arrived with a relief Parkeston Quay to Liverpool boat train. Loco changing with this train took place at Rotherwood with the loco turning on the triangle formed by the line to Retford. With the Orgreave coking plant seen behind the loco it is waiting to take over the return working which was electric hauled over the Woodhead route. The main cross-country express left Liverpool Central at 1.15pm and ran over the Cheshire Lines to Manchester Central, then round the Fallowfield Loop to the Woodhead line and Sheffield where the electric loco was replaced by steam. Continuing via Retford, Lincoln, March, Ely and Ipswich to Harwich (Parkeston Quay) where it arrived at 9.15pm to connect with the night sailing to the Hook of Holland. The loco was allocated to March MPD in March 1956 and had returned from Doncaster Works after a General overhaul in February 1958, being withdrawn in June 1960. Contemporary reports suggest that from the start of their career the riding of the B17s was inclined to be hard - in fact after 30,000 miles it has been described as rough. A characteristic of the design was its fore-and-aft oscillation, which was the outcome of the weight distribution, but the adjustment of the weights was always an extremely difficult matter. Reports suggest that weight distribution was prone to alter when fore-and-aft movement fell into phase with the piston thrust, the resulting diagonal thrust across the engine reacting seriously on the trailing axleboxes. The B17s had taken over many GC main line express workings from GC Atlantics, 4-6-0s and Director 4-4-0s in the 1930s but from 1938 heavier loadings saw A1s and V2s diagrammed for much of their work. GE section-based B17s continued to work the boat train until replaced by Britannia Pacifics in the late 1950s. *Derek Penney*

Class B17/6 4-6-0 No.61620 *Clumber* has the main Liverpool to Parkeston Quay boat train near Woodhouse on the line to Retford in August 1958. This loco would have taken over from electric traction at Sheffield Victoria. *Derek Penney*

With half a mile still to travel before reaching Sheffield Victoria from the north-west on the GC line from Manchester, Class B1 4-6-0 No.61033 *Dibatag* is crossing a bridge known locally as 'Five Arches' near Wadsley Bridge station in this view taken in 1958. *Derek Penney*

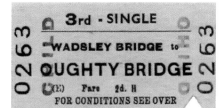

Carrying express passenger headlamps very smart Class D11/1 No. 62662 *Prince of Wales* waits for its next turn of duty outside Sheffield Victoria station c.1958. During 1912/13 the Great Central Railway's Gorton Works constructed six very large inside-cylindered 4-6-0s, the Sir Sam Fay type (GCR Class 1, LNER Class B2). Whilst these were still being built the Gorton design office was in the process of preparing drawings for a companion 4-4-0 type, the celebrated 11E Director Class (LNER D10). These were virtually a shortened version of the Sir Sam Fay 4-6-0 with their boiler diameter reduced by three inches and length by five feet. The second batch of 11 Directors was built between 1919 and 1922, six of them being named after critical battles in the First World War. These were GCR Class 11F (LNER Class D11) and differed from their predecessors in that inside admission piston valves were used which were less susceptible to leakage. These were driven from the Stephenson's link motion through rocking levers following Robinson's normal practice. At the age of 66 in 1922 John Robinson was offered the position of CME of the LNER. Declining the offer he suggested that a younger man was needed to oversee the merger which would rationalise the workshops and design facilities of the five major companies which were to be combined in the new LNER. The obvious choice for this post was Robinson's friend and CME of the GNR, Nigel Gresley who was some 20 years his junior. At Grouping in 1923, the LNER found that the North British Railway (NBR) was in urgent need of new express passenger locomotives. Gresley chose not to create a new locomotive design, but instead ordered the construction of further D11 Improved Directors. This choice may have been influenced by Robinson who was acting as a consultant to the newly formed LNER. Twenty four D11s were ordered at the end of 1923, and built within a five month period during 1924. Kitson & Co and Armstrong Whitworth & Co both built twelve. The NBR locomotives had lower cabs and boiler mountings, enabling them to fit within the relatively restrictive NBR loading gauge. Flatter domes and Gresley 'flowerpot' chimneys were fitted. They also lacked the water pickup gear which the original GCR locomotives had. The GCR locomotives were given the classification D11/1, whilst the NBR locomotives were given the classification D11/2. The NBR and GCR D11s also had contrasting names. The GCR D11s were named after GCR Directors, Royalty, and First World War battles. The NBR D11s continued a theme set by the D30s, and were named after characters in Sir Walter Scott's novels and poems. *Derek Penney*